Beyond Academic Success

Beyond Academic Success

Creating Social-Emotional Learning Balance in Elementary Students

Brett Novick

ROWMAN & LITTLEFIELD
Lanham • Boulder • New York • London

Published by Rowman & Littlefield
An imprint of The Rowman & Littlefield Publishing Group, Inc.
4501 Forbes Boulevard, Suite 200, Lanham, Maryland 20706
www.rowman.com

86-90 Paul Street, London EC2A 4NE, United Kingdom

Copyright © 2023 by Brett Novick

All rights reserved. No part of this book may be reproduced in any form or by any electronic or mechanical means, including information storage and retrieval systems, without written permission from the publisher, except by a reviewer who may quote passages in a review.

British Library Cataloguing in Publication Information Available

Library of Congress Cataloging-in-Publication Data

Names: Novick, Brett J., author.
Title: Beyond academic success : creating social-emotional learning balance in elementary students / Brett Novick.
Description: Lanham, Maryland : Rowman & Littlefield, 2023. | Includes bibliographical references. | Summary: "This book will be ideal for educators and administrators, educators, and mental health providers, and, families. The goal of the materials contained within are to develop and enrich the skills that both the educators and the pupils have in harvesting social and emotional learning within the school as well as the larger systemic community"—Provided by publisher.
Identifiers: LCCN 2023034389 (print) | LCCN 2023034390 (ebook) | ISBN 9781475861648 (cloth) | ISBN 9781475861655 (paperback) | ISBN 9781475861662 (epub)
Subjects: LCSH: Affective education. | Emotions in children. | Social skills in children. | Learning, Psychology of.
Classification: LCC LB1072 .N684 2023 (print) | LCC LB1072 (ebook) | DDC 370.15/34—dc23/eng/20230814
LC record available at https://lccn.loc.gov/2023034389
LC ebook record available at https://lccn.loc.gov/2023034390

To my late father, Dr. William Novick, who taught me how to be a father. To my parents, who taught me the importance of hard work and values. My wife, Darla, who teaches me each and every day how to be a better person, parent, and spouse. My children, Billy and Samantha, who give me hope for a future generation with pride. Also, to the many students, parents, and educators that I have had the honor of working with over the years who have taught me so very much. Please know that it has been an honor to be allowed to play a small part in their lives. The many mentors who, in both education and life, inspired me in every aspect of my life. Finally, a heartfelt thank you to the publishers and staff at Rowman & Littlefield for your confidence in publishing this book and to you, the reader, for taking precious time out of your schedule to read my book. Thank you.

Contents

Preface	ix
Introduction	xi
Chapter 1: Why Address Anger First in SEL?	1
Chapter 2: It's Not My Fault . . .: Encouraging Responsibility in Our Children	23
Chapter 3: There Is a Big World Out There: Practical SEL	41
Chapter 4: A Walk in Someone Else's Shoes . . .: Helping Students to Develop Compassion and Empathy	61
Chapter 5: What Is With All This Mindfulness?	71
Chapter 6: Conclusion	79
Notes	83
About the Author	91

Preface

Social-emotional learning (SEL) is not a new concept; it has existed in the offices of school and guidance counselors since the genesis of the profession. Counseling on how to socialize and regulate one's emotions has been the role, to at least some degree, of the counselors and social workers in schools since they began as vocational counselors in the early 1900s. Unfortunately, the services of these educational professionals had been generally restricted to those students who were referred to them or youth who behaved their way to the necessity for such services.

Then came the events at Columbine, at Virginia Tech, and at Newton, Massachusetts, and the suicide of Tyler Clementine at Rutgers University with stories of relentless bullying about his sexual orientation, and on and on. It became clear that a laser-focused approach to emotional issues was simply not enough. Rather, mental health and emotional discord needed to be broadly recognized as the public health issues they are. Further, public schools were the place to help in inoculating the next generation in these issues as almost every citizen of the next generation must pass through their doors.

This book is drawn from over 25 years of experience in working with youth, educators, and families in schools and community mental health, residential, in-home, and foster care. It has taken almost two years to write this book as this topic is so broad in focus and has roots in so many other disciplines that it is difficult to take a myopic perspective. This book could be several volumes, however, but length dilutes the vital nature of this important topic.

One aspect of SEL that we educators have realized is that it can no longer be placed on the back burner of academics. It is time to ask if a student who is academically successful but is unprepared and wilts under the light of emotional burdens or societal pressures is considered a success. For students to be successful, they must be as well-rounded as possible in this ever-changing and dynamic world.

Academics and SEL do not have to be recognized as separate disciplines. It can, and should be, infused when possible as a synergistic component of academia. Every opportunity to learn and grow is an opportunity toward the education of our students in some domain. When we discuss how we teach students, are we asking how can we teach our youth the skills necessary to succeed in the world that they will have to live and thrive in? This is the lofty component void that SEL serves to fill.

Introduction

Educating the mind without educating the heart is no education at all.

—Aristotle

As you are listening to a self-help book on relaxation and mindfulness while traveling down a busy highway, a vehicle speeds by you and cuts carelessly into your lane, just narrowly missing your left bumper. Suddenly, you are no longer thinking of taking deep, calming breaths or about that imagery of a warm, tropical beach. Now, your knuckles are clenched tightly around the steering wheel, your heart is beating out of your chest, and your eyes are squinted in a tight gaze at the vehicle that has accelerated over the hill ahead.

Words leave your lips that would make a trucker blush without the benefit of editing. Swirling around your brain are thoughts of rage and desires for terrible consequences for the negligent driver who could have taken your life in an instant. Congratulations, you just entered a realm devoid of social-emotional aptitude. This is a world where every person reacts without the benefit of self-awareness and reacts via the deeply instinctive reptilian brain of attack or be attacked.

What separates us from the other creatures of the Earth is being able to socialize and have an awareness of our wide spectrum of emotions. Yet, as in this example, sometimes we revert to a world of untamed emotion devoid of socialization proficiency. Take, for example, road rage, which has increased over the last seven years in the United States to 12,610 injuries and 218 homicides that were attributed to aggressive vehicular behaviors.[1] Clearly, when we allow emotions to run free, they can quickly get the very best (or worst) of us with dangerous consequences.

Further, we are now in a world in which we are creating children less emotionally literate than that of any generation before them. Why? Well, if we take the premise that between 60 to 90% of communication is nonverbal, as do most professionals in the field of communications, we can quickly conclude an answer.[2] In a recent survey, a majority of teenagers indicated that their favored means of socialization was texting (35%), and concurrently, less than a third of teens said they prefer chatting with friends face-to-face. Even when the opportunity presents itself for enriching socialization skills face-to-face, the same survey states that 55% of teens say that they have phones always in hand when they are spending time with peers and are thus only partially paying attention to face-to-face communication.[3]

Children literally can be walking shoulder to shoulder and deferring their communication preferences toward texting versus actually talking with each other. What does this have to do with modern public education? Yes, the 3Rs of reading, writing, and arithmetic are the perpetual yardsticks that will always be embedded in the curriculum necessary for academic success. However, if we are truly forward-thinking educators, we must also ask how we are trying to prepare our youth for the so-called "real world."

Are we getting them ready for what employers are looking for from prospective employees? Indeed.com, a top internet job-seeking site, indicates that among the top ten skills sought by employers are communication skills, teamwork abilities, and problem-solving skills. Do our youth graduate with these practical abilities, or are they ill-prepared for the world that they are inheriting? These are answers that must be considered the moment our students enter through the doors of our schools at the very earliest ages.

Not to mention, How do we teach socializing while our world was shuttered with the social distancing of our youth from 2019 to 2021? The world literally declared that our youth should be kept apart socially, and an experiment ensued of how our youth would handle being isolated to the world of technologies that they were addicted to. It may very well be years before the full social post-trauma of COVID-19 is understood, as research has only begun on this front.

Further, Are we doing our children a disservice if we do not teach them the socialization skills necessary for an ever-changing and fluid world? True, it seems the majority of youth are turning toward technology for interaction with each other; however, with social-emotional learning (SEL) skills, we can give youth a leg up on the competition that may be necessary for an ever more competitive employment atmosphere. If social skills are going the way of cursive writing curricula (which is no longer a mandate in many states), then anyone that has these coveted skills in socialization is suddenly in greater demand.

Perhaps this is why educators are turning towards SEL curricula in schools. In support of this is a study in 2018 of high school students that noted almost 90% of students who graduated from schools with a strong SEL background indicated that their peers displayed good interaction and teamwork abilities, versus a mere 46% of those in high schools with a limited SEL curriculum in place.[4] SEL also fosters positive socialization and community that can inoculate somewhat against the scourge of bullying and cyberbullying that have run rampant as a rite of passage in the history of schools of the past and present.

SEL, of course, has the dual components of both social- and emotional-learning traits. The emotional component goes hand-in-hand with that of the social aspect, and both are synergistically vital to a child's growth. An outpouring of statistics on youth shows the absolute need for addressing emotional issues. Looking at recent surveys, for instance, of adolescents and young adults indicates that issues of significant depression have risen to 13.2%.[5] Further, the National Institutes of Health indicate about 33% of teenagers will develop an anxiety disorder.[6]

Looking at this from another perspective, between 2007 and 2012, the number of youth and adolescents that have diagnosable anxiety disorders has risen a whopping 20%, and typical children are reporting more anxiety than that of psychiatric patients of the 1950s.[7]

It begs the question, What would society look like if we allowed our next generation to graduate without an iota of social-emotional learning embedded into the curriculum? It may look like a society that estimates the costs of violence of person-on-person conflict at $500 billion per year, or $5,485 per person, in the United States.[8] This is a world where playing video games that depict violence for hours on end is correlated with school delinquency, discord in school, and even violent behavior outside the realm of school.[9] Perhaps it may be similar to a World Wide Web that has ensnared at least 28% of children in so-called cyberbullying and could possibly be leading to a troubling increase in adolescent suicide that has risen to the second leading cause of death among those age 10 to 34.[10] If our goal is to have the next generation of youth inherit a better world than our own, it may take teaching how to cope better emotionally and socially in public schools to learn how to create a society better than what we inherited from those before us.

Chapter 1

Why Address Anger First in SEL?

Education is the ability to listen to almost anything without losing your temper or your self-confidence.

—Robert Frost

CHILD PROFILE

John is a 17-year-old teen who is on the verge of dropping out of high school. His teacher, Mrs. Smith, defines herself as an "old-school" teacher who lectures and demands respect and quiet in her classroom. Her classroom is so quiet that those who come into the classroom marvel that you can hear "a pin drop" in the silence of the class.

John likes to joke around and tries not to take life too seriously. His home is a place of uncomfortable silence in which all of his family tiptoes around his father's volatile moods. Without warning, his father could erupt and take aim with words or a belt with reckless abandon on anyone unfortunate to be within arm's length.

School is the only place where John feels safe to express himself without fear of being beaten down physically or emotionally. His classmate texts him the link to a video in Mrs. Smith's class, and John opens it without any idea of what is attached. For a moment, he forgets where he is and lets out a loud belly laugh at the funny viral video playing on his phone. It feels good to let loose for a moment after having to protect his mother and brothers nightly from his father's wrath.

The laughter strikes the ire of Mrs. Smith, who does not tolerate any guff or disrespect when she is teaching. "John, I will show you something funny! Get out of my classroom . . . now!" He is so thoroughly focused on the video that he does not hear his teacher's statements of growing frustration. Mrs. Smith stomps over to him and grabs the cell phone (that is also used for the many emergencies that his mother and siblings call him about). She raises her voice to almost an uncontrolled scream: "Get out now!"

Her tone snaps John back into the consciousness of the bright fluorescent lights of the classroom. As he swivels his head to face her, she continues to yell and berate him about his lack of work ethic and how "the real world will not be so funny." As he watches her yell and drops of spit fly from her mouth, he can feel a volcano of rage begin to climb up his neck and into his clenched jaws.

"F*** you!" He yells, "You b**ch . . . what do you know?" His classmates try to calm him down before he carries his tirade any further. Yet, he continues, "No! I am not going to calm down!! You are the worst teacher I have ever had . . . you are always yelling and telling us what we should do! Do you ever even stop to listen to us?"

John can hear the words spilling out of his mouth, yet they seem to be coming from a million miles away. John can discern a subtle voice at the back of his head telling him to stop and calm down, but the screaming voice in his consciousness seems to be yelling so loudly he barely perceives it. He is out of control and out of his head.

Meanwhile, Mrs. Smith is on the intercom with the main office. "You, buddy, are going to be suspended . . . get out of my class!!" John is now thrust back into the realm of consciousness as if slapped in the face.

"What?" He asks in stunned confusion.

"Grab your things and go to the main office!"

John walks out of the room without taking any of his books . . . how is he going to explain to his father that he is suspended again?

WHY ADDRESS ANGER FIRST IN SEL?

Have you ever been peacefully driving along on the highway, only to have someone cut you off and come within a hair of causing a major collision? If you have, you may have reacted in a minor (or perhaps major) fit of road rage. A verbal tirade of profanity may have been unleashed from your mouth that would make a trucker blush, before you even reacted rationally. Alternatively, you may have wished ill will upon the driver who just jeopardized your life or even given them a one-fingered salute.

WHEN ANGER HITS, IT HAS A DUAL PHYSIOLOGICAL AND PSYCHOLOGICAL IMPACT

When a perceived fight-or-flight scenario hits, your blood is diverted to your hands and feet. Literally, you are primed to not think about anything except whether to fight or flee.[1] The blood is, by design, not in your brain to fuel thinking. Pondering about the issues at hand from a social or emotional framework may well have cost our ancestors their lives in the past, as rational thinking created slower, unuseful responses when hunting and gathering.

The point is that anger essentially short-circuits one's ability for rational thinking. When the fuse in your brain that allows for social-emotional learning (SEL) has been tripped, the most evolutionary instincts of your brain for survival and fight or flight takes over. SEL will always instinctually be placed on the back burner of priorities when this is the case.

ANGER IS NOT A BAD EMOTION

Children often associate anger with rage and out-of-control behavior. This is generally because children correlate anger with rage, or rule-breaking, which is unacceptable in the classroom or in the larger scope of society. Nevertheless, anger can be the fuel that teaches students to assert themselves, set boundaries, or motivate themselves to be more productive. Hence, we have to distinguish healthy anger from the more destructive action of rage.

ANGER RUNS THE GAMBIT

Often, we attribute anger in our classrooms to an extremely reactive emotion. For instance, we classify anger as when a student throws items, directs profanity, or is physically aggressive toward others. That, however, represents one far extreme of anger. The student (or students) who displays such behavior almost always is given the undivided attention of the teacher, counselor, and (usually) the administrator.

Yet, the other pole of anger that is often less recognized is that of passive anger. That is when a student turns that same anger inward, they tend to remain quiet and withdrawn. These students simply implode into themselves versus exploding. The problem becomes that these children are often not thought of in the typical referral to school counseling or in addressing their behaviors because they are largely not seeking attention. Our objective for

SEL is for our students not to display anger but instead to do so in a manner that is both productive and assertive (see figure 1.1).

TEACHING THE DISTINCTION BETWEEN ANGER, FRUSTRATION, AND RAGE

Frustration, rage, and anger are similar yet different parts of the same animal. Yet, if our students do not know the distinction, it can be a challenge for them to develop an SEL response that is appropriate for the situation at hand. Hence, we must help them to see that anger, frustration, and rage require slightly, or at times radically, different responses when they stir inside their brains.

Anger is a common response when our students feel wronged, or cheated, or when someone has not followed the rules or respected their boundaries. It is primarily a reaction to an external factor and is generally related to something outside themselves. Frustration, on the other hand, is more of an internal process. When counseling students, we often describe it as "smad." That is a mixture of sadness because a student can't do something that they are trying to do and mad because the student can't do it despite their best efforts.[2]

NOTE ANGER AND SEL HAVE A CULTURAL COMPONENT

When we discuss anger, socialization, and emotions, we have to remember that these concepts do not occur in a vacuum. Although we tend to believe

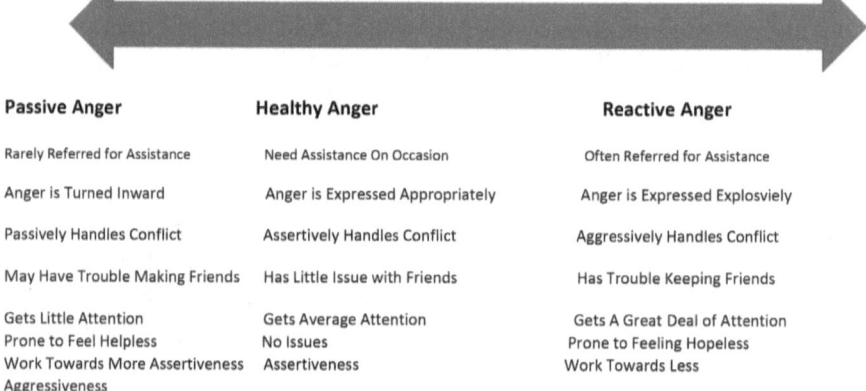

Passive Anger	Healthy Anger	Reactive Anger
Rarely Referred for Assistance	Need Assistance On Occasion	Often Referred for Assistance
Anger is Turned Inward	Anger is Expressed Appropriately	Anger is Expressed Explosviely
Passively Handles Conflict	Assertively Handles Conflict	Aggressively Handles Conflict
May Have Trouble Making Friends	Has Little Issue with Friends	Has Trouble Keeping Friends
Gets Little Attention	Gets Average Attention	Gets A Great Deal of Attention
Prone to Feel Helpless	No Issues	Prone to Feeling Hopeless
Work Towards More Assertiveness	Assertiveness	Work Towards Less Aggressiveness

Fig. 1.1. The Spectrum of Anger

that our version (the Western version) of SEL and anger is the "appropriate" means to express and understand anger, we would be very myopic in doing so. As an educator, and in society as a whole, the world is becoming ever-flattered, and we must remember that our version of SEL and anger is just one in a myriad of many. Hence, it is important to recognize how others around the world handle such concepts as anger and SEL because these are a microcosm of our students and schools as a whole.

Even cultures that are in close physical proximity to each other may handle emotions like anger vastly differently. For instance, in China, it is acceptable for people to express anger with yelling and reactive emotion.[3] Meanwhile, in Japan, it is considered unacceptable and a breach of etiquette to lose your temper. That being said, Japan has a wide range of words to voice varying forms of anger.[4] Even symbols such as "the middle finger" or other symbols of insult are quite contradictory depending on varying cultures.[5]

PREPARATION FOR ANGER, FRUSTRATION, AND STRESS

Despite most of our schools having gymnasiums and physical education classes to address the physical health of our students, most of our schools lack a set, controlled, environment to tackle the emotional and mental health needs of an increasingly anxious, stressed, and frustrated generation. When a student is trying to escape the turmoil of emotional discord or anxiety, the question in the school is about where they should go. Often a classroom is an overstimulating environment of no escape.

The goal of a reset room, "Zen Den," or mindfulness room is to provide that space to decompress and relax. It is differentiated from a "time-out" room in which students, in the latter case, are brought to a relatively bare room with the intention of de-escalation of tantrums, anger, or out-of-control behaviors. The reset room should not be looked at as a place of calm and serenity. If a school does not have a room that they can designate solely for this purpose, an area set aside in a classroom can suffice, provided the room is not overly noisy.

An elementary reset room should include the following:[6]

- Crayons, markers, and so on.
- Allow a student to express emotions in an alternate way aside from verbally.
- Calming music and dim lights to foster a relaxing setting.
- Avoid fluorescent lighting, as bright lights can be an obstacle to relaxation.

- Comfortable seating (bean bag chairs, reclining chairs, and so on).
- Manipulatives that allow students to be distracted and redirect focus.
- Carpets that students can lie down on comfortably.
- Place of quiet reflection.
- Not a place of punishment or consequence.

FRUSTRATION AND LEARNED HELPLESSNESS

When a student says that they "can't do something or everyone hates them," for instance, they begin walking down the road of learned helplessness in the classroom and in life. Why? Because the general response that they are hoping to receive is a confirmation from adults that "they can do it," or "I will like you." These seem like innocuous and well-intentioned responses; however, this keeps the solution to frustration outside the locus of a student's control. That is, they are always looking outside themselves for validation and support.

As this continues to occur, the student will continue to look toward something, or someone, outside of themselves for confirmation that they can do a task or succeed in life, in general. So what is the response to a student who exclaims, "I can't do it," or "No one likes me"? This thought process can lead to helplessness and anxiety and/or can create an atmosphere of hopelessness and depressive traits when prolonged in one's thinking.[7] The educator can ask them to debate that unuseful thought process by asking, "Tell me three things you were able to do today," or "Who are three students in the class that like and are friendly with you?"

It is not enough for a student to think about what they thought without challenging its validity. The difficulty with thoughts and children is that because they think something, they deem it 100% as truth.[8] Younger children tend to have fantasy thinking in which they believe that what happens in the world is somehow *caused* by what they think.[9] For instance, an old childhood rhyme used to be "Step on a crack and you'll break your mother's back." This is a prime example of a child's cause-and-effect thinking.

CLASSROOM/EDUCATIONAL APPLICATION OF ADDRESSING FRUSTRATION AND AVOIDING LEARNED HELPLESSNESS

The "Real World Rules" often seem so commonsensical that it would seem that they do not even have to be reviewed with students. That being said, it is because we as adults have been immersed in that so-called real world for so long that its edicts seem all too commonplace for most of us. If we were from another culture or did not have adult experience, these items would suddenly be foreign and difficult for us to grasp.

REAL-WORLD CLASSROOM RULES

As educators, our job is to look toward teaching potential consequences in a parallel (yet diluted) fashion for the so-called "real world." To avoid the specter of learned helplessness and frustration, a student must recognize what is firmly within their locus of control.

For instance:

1. **If you hurt someone's feelings . . . No empty apologies:** An apology must include how you plan to correct the wrongdoing that was made. No knee-jerk reactive apologies are accepted.
2. **If you want someone to play with you . . . Ask:** It is not the responsibility of the teacher, your peers, or your parents to set up social time. If someone rejects playing with the student, what does the student have as an alternate plan of who to spend time with?
3. **If you say you are going to do it . . . Do it:** You are responsible for doing what you say you are going to do or explaining why you were not able to do so directly to the person you disappointed. If you do not do your work, you will have to do it at some time that is not of your liking or choosing.
4. **If you break it:** Do your best to fix it, whether it be property or classroom/peer relationships.
5. **If you are angry or sad:** When a student has tantrums or sulks, this is an ineffective manner of demonstrating anger or sadness. Therefore, a student must express some ideas of what may work to remedy the problem.
6. **If you make a decision:** Making a decision should be funneled through several cognitive filters before it is made. As educators, we can ask our students the following to make good decisions.
    a. Is it kind?
        i. Does everyone find what you are doing kind? Or are you singling out one student to tease?
        ii. Do you think it is true?
            - Like any other community, rumors and gossip can spread like wildfire in schools and be fanned by the winds of social media. If you are uncertain if it is true, do not say it.

- This is especially important for more gullible students, who are often used as "messengers" for gossip or making actions that their peers may want to say but not want the negative disciplinary consequences for spreading such information.
  b. Would saying this make your teacher or parent proud?
    i. As educators, if we do not make some manner of lasting influence on our students, we have not fulfilled our role. Having students utilize our influence over them provides a more lasting impression in the SEL realm. Hence, students should ask themselves if the statement they are about to say is in alignment with what their parents and teacher would think is acceptable.

TATTLING VERSUS TELLING

Students that are extreme rule followers will sometimes become tattlers in an attempt to make certain everyone follows the same rules in a rigid fashion. This can lead those same students to be isolated from peers who do not want them to "rat" on them and get them into trouble with adults. Students who try to maintain a grip on every rule of their peers can quickly be labeled as a "tattletale."

It is helpful for students to realize and separate tattling (which is unnecessary) from telling (which is needed for everyone's safety). Telling should always be deferred to an adult, while telling should be attempted to be remedied individually by students first.

Here is a table to help students decipher the two.

Table 1.1

Tattling	Telling
Someone cuts in line in front of me	Bullying/cyberbullying
Minor arguments	Physical fights
Someone not sharing	Someone trying to use/encourage substance use
Someone not wanting to spend time with you	Someone "daring" someone to do something dangerous
Boredom	Encouraging the keeping of secrets from parents or educators could be dangerous

HOW DO WE SHOW AGREEMENT IN THE "REAL WORLD"?

Having students sign that they understand the real-world classroom rules. Why sign the rules? Because it is how any significant commitment occurs in the real world of society via contracts for a whole host of vital functions and agreements. Additionally, a signed contract can be pointed to when a student fails or refuses to take responsibility for an action that they had agreed to adhere to certain rules and regulations.

NOT BEING ABLE TO FACE REJECTION OR CONSEQUENCES MAKES STUDENTS MORE SUSCEPTIBLE TO FRUSTRATION AND ANGER

Modern society has shifted toward insulating children from the potential consequences of their actions or potential rejection. Of course, no one likes to see a child struggle, fail, or be hurt in any way. Yet, failure, and that experience of a modicum of hardship, is precisely the necessary catalyst for a child to strengthen their social-emotional wings toward increased growth.

Further, failing initially and some degree of rejection encourages our students to redirect their SEL sails, build a modicum of frustration tolerance, and learn the discipline to try again.[10] When a student has limited failure, rejection, or the natural consequences of a poor choice, they ultimately build tolerance in these domains only after the stakes are higher as adolescents or young adults from the much-less-forgiving rules of the so-called "real world." It is a supposed inoculation from the challenge that society has in store for them in the near future.

When these consequences do come to roost, many students at the secondary level who don't learn how to handle anger reactively strike out at the perceived unfairness of the world around them. Anger supersedes SEL constructs because their previous childhood world was one of entitlement and lack of need to navigate through the society around them. Hence, those who burst the imagined bubble of a life filled only with comfort that has been built around them are left to feel the wrath and a lack of need or ability to regulate societal skills.

Even still, our current world does not always lend itself to learning the emotional regulations necessary to foster a strong SEL skill set. For instance, let's look at the current mindset some have that everyone should *earn* an award for participation in a given school or sporting activity. In theory, it sounds like a generous gesture: everyone is recognized, everyone is happy, and everyone succeeds. Yet, the so-called "real world" has a very different set of standards.

In society, only a select few are rewarded for their efforts, and the majority are destined to be left out at some point in school, work, sports, or friendships. This is not necessarily bad because it helps students find their strengths and work toward these abilities accordingly. As educators, we must help students to recognize that all of us have strengths and areas that we will always work hard to get better at. It is not accurate to tell students as they grow that they are going to be great at everything because this is simply untrue. A student may struggle with math, athletics, or another area, which is acceptable. What is not acceptable is for educators to focus only on weaknesses.

Further, those students who have practiced social-emotional discipline understand that the world has a focus less on the individual and more on society as a whole. Hence, they are less impacted every time the world does not cater to them only as an individual. They are less apt to react in anger and self-pity and more likely to be on the road to successful development. These children become more driven to try even harder, realign their SEL compass to note what they may improve upon, and muster the strength to go in another direction if necessary. This is akin to what we might call emotional maturity.

CLASSROOM ACTIVITY

- Read age-appropriate biographies about how real-life persons were handed obstacles and maneuvered them in a gracious and productive manner.
- Role-play on how to handle scenarios when things do not go your way.
- Look at poor examples of sportsmanship/losing, and discuss them in a morning meeting format.
- Discuss in organized sports how both teams congratulate each other on a "good game," regardless of the outcome.

FOCUSING ON STRENGTHS AND ACKNOWLEDGING WEAKNESSES

Think about when you have taken a test and get it back; what is the first thing you look at? If you are like most of us, it is the grade first, followed by what you got wrong. We are primed to focus on the weaknesses and the mistakes; we even call mathematics questions "problems." When we provide support to students, we are looking to shore up deficiencies, and sometimes inadvertently, the subtle message is you need to change to be a good student. Tom

Rath says it best in his best-selling book *Strengthsfinder 2.0*: "You cannot be anything you want to be but you can be a lot more of who you already are."[11] In our classes, it is always best to harness the SEL strengths of our students versus trying to go upstream by focusing on weaknesses.

HOW DO YOU GET TO REACHING EMOTIONAL MATURITY IN THE CLASSROOM?

Reaching emotional maturity in a classroom means a student can recognize and utilize their personal strengths in SEL. Additionally, there is also the recognition that they are part of an intricate societal web that does not focus on them but is part of a much greater and grander picture.

1. **It is not all about me:** It is an extremely age-typical behavior for early elementary students to be egocentric, believing that the world, and everything that happens in it, revolves around something they do or do not do. As children emotionally mature, they should begin to recognize the center of control of the world has much less to do with them.[12] Asking how their behavior impacts the other students and their academic society offers a shift from egocentrism toward societal empathy and away from empty, negative attention-seeking behaviors.
2. **Being able to be proactive:** The more tools a student has in their proverbial toolbox, the more likely they are able to handle new and novel situations. Often, we ask students to come up with "a solution" for an SEL issue. One of the confusing aspects of SEL is that a seemingly similar problem in the future may require a completely different solution. A perfect example, as part of the humor in *The Big Bang Theory*, is when the main character, Sheldon, tries a single social intervention that is often clumsy or ill-fitted but he continues with that same behavior despite its obvious lack of efficacy.[13]

    Hence, asking for several potential solutions allows a student to develop numerous solutions that can be carried over to similar SEL situations in which one SEL response may not work and requires the use of a secondary, or even a tertiary, solution. Students with limited skill sets try those restricted skills more aggressively versus shifting to another skill. As Abraham Maslow once said, "To the man who only has a hammer, everything looks like a nail." For a student who has limited social skills, they will try to hammer everything regardless of what is around them.

3. **Asking questions and getting answers:** If you ask a younger elementary student if they have a question, you will most likely get a statement or a story versus an actually formulated inquiry. For instance, a question will lead down a rabbit hole of stories versus the seeking of information by the student to find an answer or learn more about the topic/person they are speaking with. Therefore, we have to set up the context for a question. If a student is going to truly ask a question, they must know it will start with a sentence starter of "who," "what," "when," "why," "where," or "how."
4. **Asking for attention versus behaving for attention:** Students who want attention can do it in two ways—behaving toward it or asking for it. The SEL effective class rewards the student who asks for it appropriately with verbal praise and positive energy within their educational society. The class that places a great deal of attention on negative attention-seeking tends to feed more of this maladaptive societal behavior within the classroom setting. Remember, it is always easier to do negative behavior than positive.

    Think of it this way: If you are growing a garden, do you want to water and fertilize the flowers or the weeds? The answer, of course, is hopefully the flowers, and you do this by giving them attention by religiously watering and fertilizing them. You may spray weed killer on the weeds; however, you certainly are not watering or fertilizing them. Why? Because you want to give your energy and time to the items you want to grow.

    Now let's think of a classroom setting. Those students who exhibit appropriate SEL traits are all likely to get equal amounts of attention from the teacher. The student who goes against the grain of SEL may, in fact, garner a great deal more attention, emotion, and faculty trying to quell his/her emotional outbursts. It is not that they don't want to address these issues, obviously; however, we should address these negative behaviors and concerns with the very least amount of effort, attention, and faculty possible to avoid feeding what we do not want.
5. **Alternate opinions are acceptable:** Students can have a very black-and-white view of opinions. As children learn their role as students, they are indoctrinated into the notion of answers being strictly right or wrong. The notion of a topic being in neither category (i.e., in a so-called "gray area") can be a challenging concept to grasp. Yet, opinions can indeed be not right or wrong because they are based upon preferences.
    a. **Use writing for opinions:** Using the concept of writing helps students to expound upon what their opinion is and why they lean toward this concept.

b. **What do you like?** When we discuss items such as what a student likes and dislikes, we get the idea that opinions are not a linear concept. Rather, we can have similarities and differences. Further, a peer's "opinion" is not necessarily right or wrong; it just is.
c. **Use of "I" messages:** "I" messages are simply a format for which a student can state an opinion:
   i. I feel _____ (How do you feel?)
   ii. Because _____ (Why do you feel that way?)
   iii. So I _____ (What supports your opinion?)
d. **Is it right, is it wrong, or is it an opinion?** Having students discuss if an opinion is "right or wrong" is a way to help students understand that one's opinions are simply one's personal preferences. For example, Is it "right or wrong" that I like pizza, video games, or a certain TV show? When a student begins to recognize they cannot classify the gray-area concept of opinions, they begin to understand the deeper meaning of one's opinions.
e. **We can share similar opinions**: In terms of opinions, it is important in SEL that we discuss if we share similar opinions with peers. Why? Because those with similar opinions and interests are those that we tend to gravitate to as friends. Hence, a discussion of agreement/disagreement with opinions is a vital SEL skill as well. Also, opinions are not right or wrong and are a gray area, which is another important concept to grasp in the SEL domain.
f. **We can agree to disagree:** It is important that our students can try to understand and empathize from another's perspective. It is also, concurrently, just as important that we can try to understand another's opinion without subscribing, or agreeing, to what another's opinion may be. Opinion is about listening, not necessarily agreeing.
g. **I can agree to disagree with another's opinions by:**
   i. **Staying calm:** Teaching our students to disagree while staying calm is perhaps the best lesson we can teach them and is productive for having conversations and debates.
   ii. **Avoiding personal attacks:** It is important that they can disagree with the other student without being disagreeable and insulting the other student's personality, character, or dignity.
   iii. **Utilization of "I" statements:** See previous examples earlier in the reading.
   iv. **Look for points you agree upon or are helpful:** Many of us tend to discount all of our opinions if we don't agree with points of it that are distasteful to us. Help students find some points that they find positive or useful in a conversation or opinion from which they can then create a productive conversation.

SIMPLE CONVERSATION STARTERS

Conversation starters are much akin to writing prompts in the classroom. The point is that they are a foundation from which to build. The goal is that they are noncontroversial, universal to most student experiences, and can build a conversation. The following are some simple conversation starters for students to develop from. Further conversation starters can be found in any number of free conversation-starter applications on smartphones and computer devices:

1. What are your favorite things to do with your friends?
2. What do you think of the weather?
3. What is your favorite movie? Why?
4. What is your favorite video game? Game to play? Television show? Why?

Conversation Starters on the Telephone

With many of our students used to using texting as their primary form of social communication, a phone call can create a great deal of anxiety. Working with students in the classroom from a script can help in developing skills that will be necessary for interacting with others, calling for a job, or securing a play date.

The following is an example of a script to help students rehearse when making a telephone call:

1. Who is it I am calling?
2. Why do I want to call them?
3. What do I need to tell them?
4. Is there anything I need to write down?
5. Do I have a pen and paper ready and available?
6. What should I say if the person is not there?
7. What happens if I get voicemail? If I get the voicemail, then:
    a. Hello, it's _____
    b. I was calling because I needed/wanted to _____
    c. Please call me back at _____
    d. Thank you
    e. Goodbye

Topics to Avoid in Conversation

Unfortunately, sometimes students learning SEL skills that are engaging in conversation gravitate to topics that lead down a path of conflict and discord. Hence, it is best that students stay away from the following topics when initially talking with peers and others:

- Religion
- Politics
- Bragging about themselves
- Bodily functions/"bathroom talk"
- Medical or mental health issues

CONFUSION QUESTIONS VERSUS STATEMENTS

In especially younger elementary students, or those who are concrete thinkers, questions are often confused for statements and stories. In other words, when asked, "Does anyone have any questions?" they are likely to continue on a long tirade of stories or statements. Being that questions are the way that conversations evolve into dialogue, it is vital that a student distinguish a question from a statement.

The following are helpful in this regard:

1. Questions are not statements.
2. Questions should begin with "who," "what," "when," "where," "why," or "how."
3. Questions may involve nonverbal cues as well as verbal cues.
4. Teach inflection in verbalization to indicate the asking of a question.
5. Ask questions and encourage questions.
6. Rehearse questions versus statements by looking at television, videos, and other appropriate scenarios for modeling.

ANOTHER SEL CLASSROOM ACTIVITY ON OPINIONS

Present a list of items that are preferences, such as foods, television shows, sports, and games. Discuss with students why they feel a certain way about this preference. Have students ask questions about why their peers have this opinion and discuss listening and understanding versus discounting and refusing to understand the other's perspective.

MORE ON SOCIAL REJECTION ... USING THE SAME TOOL UNTIL IT BREAKS

Let's go back to Abraham Maslow and the hammer analogy discussed earlier; if a student gets rejected from a peer group, due to the harsh reality of life on the playground, what is he/she left to do? There are many options on the playground of life to consider. Yet, students with lower SEL skills often restrict their options, as we will see in the following paragraphs. They will "hammer" because it is all they know.[14]

One option is to simply try to *force/pry/hammer* themselves upon the students who reject them. Many students with poor SEL skills choose this option; doing so often leads to further social rejection, frustration, and then potential disciplinary consequences. When they are repeatedly not accepted, they use the same limited toolset but do so harder and more forcefully. They will hammer until the proverbial nail breaks, or they are tired of striking with the hammer.

When they choose the option of hammering and prying, however, the tunnel vision and sting of rejection block out the possibility of considering socializing with the numerous other students who are on the playground, at lunch, or in class. These alternative peers are much more likely to readily accept invitations to socialize because they are not previously engaged like the group that the student is trying to force themselves into. In short, they miss out on targeting those they could most likely socialize with.

If this lesson is not learned, the student may well continue to crumple into a flaming ball of anger, frustration, and self-pity each time a social situation comes into view that they are rejected from. These children have difficulty recognizing that in any social situation, there are subtle, unspoken rules that must be adopted for socializing.

For instance, on the playground, the following tacit "rules" exist:

1. When we have begun a game or activity, another student may not join until we are done with the designated activity.
2. Every such activity has a natural starting and ending time in which another student may then enter this circle of activity (i.e., watch what happens when a parent tries to pull the plug in the middle of a child's video game).
3. One exception is that some leeway may be provided for students who are popular or have exceptional SEL skills and can navigate these subtle rule systems.

FAIR IS A LINEAR CONCEPT: EVERYONE GETS THE SAME EXACT THING, OR IT IS LABELED "UNFAIR"

The lower the SEL skills, the more students tend to shift toward black-and-white thinking (this is also called literal or concrete thinking). Younger students, and those with lessened SEL traits, tend to look at fairness as a linear concept. That is, they see fairness as meaning everyone gets the same thing equally. Their anger thus is fueled by a belief that the world, the school, or their teacher is unfair because others have something, or got something, that they do not have.

Of course, such a linear view of fairness is not an effective means in a school or society at large.[15] If linear fairness was the way of the world, it wouldn't matter if your students needed extra help with math or reading. You would provide them all with the same exact manner of teaching and never make exceptions for those that needed help in a particular subject area. Fair would mean everyone gets the *same* manner of treatment and intervention. The classroom would be taught in a "one-size-fits-all" approach that would help some, and hinder others, in the name of equality. A discussion should ensue in class about the ridiculous nature of attempting to treat everyone identically regardless of need.

CLASSNESS LINEAR FAIRNESS QUESTIONS TO ASK

1. What would happen if everyone was treated exactly the same?
2. What would it be like if all people were exactly the same?
3. If we all had the exact same job, what would happen?
4. How do we make sure everything is fair in our classroom?

EMPATHY IS NOT ALWAYS A NATURAL SKILL

Often, when one discusses divorce with children, the time-tested advice is to assure a child that the divorce is not their fault.[16] Now, as adults, we recognize divorce to be primarily an adult issue. Yet children, developmentally, start off believing that anything that happens in their world is due to something they have done/not done. Hence, they are egocentric and look at the world with themselves at the very center.

Putting yourself at the center of every action is almost the exact opposite of empathy. In fact, one may call that "self-centeredness," which can be a barrier to the SEL foundation of understanding another.[17] As a child matures, as we stated earlier, they begin to see the world operate primarily outside their sphere of influence. At this point, empathy begins to develop, emotional maturity begins to take hold, and, thus, SEL traits begin to emerge.

DRAMA AND ATTENTION-SEEKING DON'T GENERALLY WORK IN THE SOCIETY OF THE PLAYGROUND

Some students have learned from experience that they can seek maximum adult attention by crying or sulking as the focus shifts primarily to them and away from others when they are at home. These same students expect to draw the attention of their peers, thinking they may ask, "What is the matter . . . Are you okay??" This generally has little impact in the playground society, as most children quickly move on to activities with other peers, creating further frustration for the student who initially attempted to seek attention in this matter.

If a child wants attention, we must teach them that they must specifically ask for it and verbalize what they need. The idea of sulking or pouting is an ineffective manner of socializing because it does not tell those around you what you need to remedy the problem at hand. In other words, if you seek someone to play with you, it requires the courage to ask versus drawing them to you by sulking, pouting, or other similar negative attention-seeking behavior(s).

HANDICAPPED SOCIAL SKILLS

Today's students are focused on the glow of a smartphone screen like moths to a flame. It is the contemporary contradiction of modern-day communication; children are socializing with ever more peers with less quality in those very interactions and increased feelings of depression, anxiety, and negative self-image.[18] Our students now have a far greater network of peers that they can interact with and do so in a far more superficial manner. Modern childhood interactions and conversations are often much shallower, briefer, and less complete than only a generation past.

At issue is the fact that a vital portion of the dialogue in modern exchanges is sorely lacking; that of experiencing full face-to-face communication. Communication is so very much more than the words we speak on a daily basis. Research indicates that only 7% of any message is conveyed through our actual words, 38% is how we phrase things, and a full 55% is via our body language.[19] What does this denote for communications in the modern era? This means that our students are not practicing or developing over 50% of those traits necessary for understanding the full spectrum of communication.[20] Without the ability to understand body language or the way things are phrased, they often misunderstand, misread, or otherwise misinterpret conversations among themselves and others. It is like trying to learn a foreign language and understanding only about half of what is being said. This means that a child is left trying to fill in the gaps in the dialogue with their best guess of what the other child is trying to say.

LOSS OF FLUENCY IN NONVERBAL COMMUNICATION GENERATES ANGRY AND FRUSTRATED STUDENTS

With students using technology as the primary means of conversing, the importance of nonverbal traits is often forgotten. Thus the question often becomes that if a student receives a text, or sees a social media post, how does the child interpret the message? Does the student see it as one that is sarcastic, serious, funny, insulting, hostile, or complementary? That question is often left up for clarification in the mind of the youth. Unfortunately, children (and adults) are notoriously bad at interpreting interactions without the benefit of seeing nonverbal cues.

How bad? Even close friends and married adults average only 35% in being able to accurately discern the intentions or feelings of the person closest to them. "Almost no one ever scores higher than 60% (in this test)," reports psychologists William Ickes and Marianne Mast, founders of empathic accuracy studies, at the University of Texas at Arlington.[21] If this refers to adults with seemingly years of wisdom, what of students without experience in conversational and social skills? The assumption is that this group almost certainly will rank even lower in the interpretation of the texts and social media of their peers.

Consequently, what becomes of the thousands of brief texts, messages, or dialogue that are obscure in the intention that our students may see on a weekly basis? Children, much like adults, tend to look toward the negative side of unclear communication. For instance, think about the very worst thing that your parents ever said to you as a child. Now, alternatively, what was the most hurtful statement by a peer when you were in school? Now, shift gears for a moment, and think of the kindest statement made to you by your parents or peers. Which is easier to recall?

If you are like most of us, you will tend to most quickly remember the negative comments, which stick in your brain and outlast other memories. In fact, Dr. Teresa M. Amabile, director of research at the Harvard Business

School, analyzed some 12,000 diary entries and determined that "the negative effect of a setback at work on happiness was more than twice as strong as the positive effect of an event that signaled progress. The power of a setback to increase frustration is over three times as strong as the power of progress to decrease frustration."[22] Thus the power of negativity tends to have a far greater impact than the pull of positive interactions in self-esteem, social media, and beyond.

Clearly, our students are going to continue to employ social media as their primary means of communication. It has become ingrained into the fabric of most children's social life and continues to be more so with each successive year of this next generation. So, how do we ensure that they use this medium to provide clear dialogue?

LESSONS IN POSITIVE AND PRODUCTIVE COMMUNICATION IN THE CLASSROOM AND BEYOND

1. **Don't Assume Others Can Read Between the Lines:** Often, it is human nature to tell another what you "don't want." The issue is anyone telling what they "don't" want never provides any constructive details of what one needs or wants. For instance, a student indicating, "I don't want to do my math," does not state what they want to do or what they may need. In all classrooms, interactions avoid the word "don't" and replace it with "do." If we use "do," one is providing information on what we need the other party to provide us with.
2. **Repeat What Someone Has Said if You Are Not Sure:** In counseling, a concept called reflective listening is a common foundational skill of communication. Basically, it involves repeating what the other person had said to be certain you are clear in its meaning and intention. Teaching students to repeat what another has said and then questioning if they understood it correctly can help avoid conflict due to misunderstanding or the (all-too-common) issue of not listening in the first place.
3. **Again, Those "I" Statements**: A student telling a peer how they feel emotionally, why they feel that way, and what they need is the foundation for assertive communication. Without these three traits, another student/teacher is left to try to mindread, which leads quickly to communication breakdowns socially. The statement is also a means of developing a solution-based method for problems from the outset.
4. **The Volume of One's Communication:** Some of our shy students tend to have a voice tone so low that those around them simply ignore their requests. Others are so unintentionally loud that peers stay away

socially because they equate increased volume with potential anger. A good manner of regulating volume is to practice with "remote control." Have students try a low/loud voice and then pretend to use an old television remote control to pretend to regulate their voices until it is at a good volume appropriate for dialogue.

5. **Smile While Conversing:** As we discussed earlier, for a number of reasons, it may be a challenge for students to read the emotional feedback from a peer or have the courage to start a conversation. Teaching students to smile during conversation will allow peers to recognize that others are open to dialogue and appear less threatening in nature.

Chapter 2

It's Not My Fault . . .

Encouraging Responsibility in Our Children

In the final analysis, the one quality that all successful people have is the ability to take on responsibility.

—Michael Korda

CHILD PROFILE

Danny is an 18-year-old who jokes that he is addicted to playing video games. He does not actually have any friends who visit but has hundreds of "friends" that he plays games with from all over the world via the internet. Danny's mother is concerned because he appears overweight from drinking too many sodas and eating the candy bars that he has stashed next to his video game system in a mini-fridge.

His room is scattered with the wrappers of the various candy bars littered along with a mosaic of discarded soda cans on a deeply soiled carpet. Whenever he decides to, he comes down for dinner or makes himself any of his favorite prepackaged meals that his mother keeps fully stocked.

Danny talks to his parents only when he wants a new video game or needs money for something. He knows that any lengthy conversation will lead to his parents bugging him to get a job, which will seriously cut into his video game time and web surfing. Danny does not see a reason to get a job that he likely won't enjoy anyway. He sits reclined on his soft bed, puts on the new pair of headphones his parents got him, and sees which of his friends are online to play the next round of his favorite video game.

TEACHING A CHILD TO RIDE THE BIKE OF LIFE

Remember those days long ago when you learned the childhood ritual of riding a bike? At first, your parents held the bicycle tightly and trotted alongside you as you took your first wobbling, unsteady pedals. As you became more confident, they ran a little faster and, eventually, let you go. You peddled, swaying along, uncertain at first but building more and more confidence with each push of the pedal.

As your parents, they warned you of the dangers and made sure you wore your helmet and kneepads. They steadied and straightened your direction when you focused on looking at the pedals and drifted toward the danger of the impending curbs. Yes, you may have fallen, had the occasional scraped knee, and shed a few tears. However, your parents always dusted you off, cleaned your wounds, and put you back on the right path. In short, your parents carefully balanced your safety with your burgeoning desire for independence.

So is the analogy for educators in developing a child's character and motivation. We must carefully mix the blending of freedom, security, and student growth. In doing so, we keep our students moving in the right direction on the road of life while giving them the subtle nudges they may need from the harsh, and unforgiving, concrete curbs of the world.[1]

OUR STUDENTS MAY BE COMING FROM AN ALL-INCLUSIVE VACATION

Picture that you have been offered an all-inclusive vacation. Such a vacation provides unlimited food, entertainment, internet, and even butler service. The objective is that you do not have to lift a finger; it is all done for you without you even having to communicate a need or exercise even a modicum of patience. How much might you pay for this trip? A thousand dollars? Five thousand? What if I told you that you could be at the resort for the next 18-plus years without paying a dime or offering any contributions? Now . . . doesn't that sound like a virtual paradise?

This is sometimes what occurs for students that do not learn the habit of responsibility in their childhood. They are provided with all the items they could ever need or want without having to earn, negotiate, or work toward establishing rewards. In turn, they do not learn to develop motivation, patience, or an ability to deal with the frustration of delayed gratification. Imagine if you flash forward 18 years and you have an "adult child" who continues to sit and play endless video games, is unemployed, and is mindlessly munching bag after bag of chips. The parent is left asking, "Why is the child like this?" Yet, a more accurate inquiry may be, "Why would they be like this?"

Further, these students in school do not have the patience to socialize or deal emotionally. Why? Because the ability to act in a disciplined manner, experience frustration, or delay gratification simply was never tested, built, or challenged.

THE EPIDEMIC OF "HELICOPTERING"

A relatively recent epidemic of parenting styles is known as the "helicopter" parent. A helicopter parent is considered one who "hovers" over their child's every move and fulfills their every need (whether the child needs it or not).[2] In doing so, the parent micromanages everything the child does, looks for what other students do to their child with an eye toward protecting their child from hurt, and looks for every opportunity to make certain they are always needed by their son or daughter. This becomes an issue for the child who is trying to grow into society due to the following concerns:

1. As our students grow, the role of an adult is to pull back as the students mature and allow them to test their abilities toward independence. Helicopter parenting simply will not provide this flexibility and stave opportunities for growth and independent socialization.
2. The "helicoptering" style sends a subtle message to students that they cannot do anything without the help of others. The child begins to falsely believe the focus of the child's behavioral control and self-esteem as something that is outside of themselves. Therefore, they are constantly looking towards others to fill the vacuum of emptiness left by not feeling whole or capable of success. Therefore, they are constantly looking toward others to fill the vacuum of emptiness left by not feeling whole or capable of success.

THE 3 RS: READING, 'RITING, AND RESPONSIBILITY

Teaching responsibility is vital in a classroom setting. The ability of a student to take responsibility for positive behaviors and academic successes is readily achieved. However, it may be a far more important lesson for them to take responsibility for what they did (or did not) do to honestly earn a lower grade or confess to less-than-stellar behaviors. For instance, when they fail, do they blame others? Do they subtly accuse the teacher or peers? Or do they simply turn on themselves or behave apathetically?

It is vital for classroom conversations on responsibility and accepting the dual nature of accepting the positive as well as the negative behaviors that a student may encounter in the classroom setting. Taking responsibility for doing poorly shows a far better comprehension of SEL skills than the latter, for it displays the maturity of taking responsibility.

To be effective, teaching responsibility must be done in a clear, concise, and nonemotional manner school-wide. Why? Because in the real world, if one does 80 mph in a 65 mph zone in one part of the state, the law is relatively the same in another part. This means that you have some idea of consistency in terms of what should be your responsibility and the potential consequences of violating these boundaries.

In a school, if a student chews gum in Mrs. Ahmed's class, do they get a similar consequence as if they chew gum in Mr. Rodrigues's classroom? If these consequences are not at least somewhat similar, it becomes much harder to learn responsibilities. For SEL behaviors to be learned, rewards and consequences cannot vary from classroom to classroom in the same academic environment.

THE GOLDEN RULE OF RESPONSIBILITY

When we do anything that our students can do for themselves, we effectively disable them and the SEL skills that they are developing. The subtle message that we are teaching them is, "You are not capable of doing this on your own . . . you do need my help." This leads, in turn, to self-esteem issues and/or overreliance on others for help. In modern education, it is extremely difficult not to push a student along when they are lagging behind due to the tides of increasing academic demands in public education upon educators and students alike.

That being said, as Henry Ford once said, "If you think you can do a thing or think you can't do a thing, you're right." In terms of teaching, if you tell a student directly or subtly they can't do something . . . "you're right." We have taught them the concept of "learned helplessness." A psychological term for this is, quite simply put, learning that throwing in the towel is more effective than trying because the consequence is always predictable and you can be disappointed if you don't try.

THE MARSHMALLOW EXPERIMENT ON RESPONSIBILITY... NOT JUST FLUFF

In the 1970s, psychologist Walter Mischel at Stanford University conducted a series of experiments on responsibility.[3] The concept of the test was relatively straightforward, in that a child was offered a choice between having a single marshmallow now or two marshmallows if they were able to wait until the researcher returned. The researcher would then leave the room for 15 minutes, and when they returned (if the marshmallow was still intact), the child would be given two marshmallows to reward their patience. How does this relate to students and responsibility?

As it turns out, these same children were followed into adulthood, and it was established that those youth who were able to generate the responsibility of disciplining themselves to wait for the two marshmallows had greater SAT scores, better educational success as adults, lower body mass indexes, and many of the other attributes necessary for social and emotional success.[4] The bottom line is that the younger a child can establish responsibility and self-discipline, the better a chance to sculpt success as a socially and emotionally competent adult.

WHAT EXACTLY CAN WE DO TO APPLY THE MARSHMALLOW EXPERIMENT, SEL, AND STUDENT SUCCESS?

One of the most vital skills that students can learn and exhibit on the road to success is perseverance. Any worthwhile skill, such as social-emotional learning, is directly correlated with the amount of time, focus, and patience that they can direct to reaching the objective at hand.[5] Evermore, however, students' concentration is being evaporated by youth voluntarily subjecting themselves to only quick soundbites of technology that only encourage very short periods of focus before they swipe it away in favor of the next video, game, or experience.

So the question becomes the following: How do we build perseverance and discipline skills for a student to be successful in school and society? To build discipline and perseverance, it is important to gradually increase the amount of time a student focuses on a task. If we are working on skills like concentration and mindfulness, we can start with only a few minutes and gradually build this over time. The importance is in setting aside a small amount of deliberate time each day for the discipline at hand (such as learning how to socialize and deal with emotions). Of course, perseverance is a life skill necessary in academics, vocation, and relationships as well.

In our society, we tend to reward the end result (i.e., grades and output), and we miss the vital nature of the effort. Yet, it is in the struggle and discipline that students develop patience and the ability to succeed in the most challenging of tasks. Hence, in SEL and in the classroom at large, the celebration of a student's effort versus success is a means of bolstering discipline and the desire to persevere.[6] Such concepts as becoming self-aware, a key SEL and mindfulness concept, is something that takes a lifetime of perseverance to fully embrace and does not have a definitive conclusion. Talking to our students as to how success and failure are relative terms can also further assist in understanding one's self-awareness.

This is not to say we should not celebrate success. Rather, make certain that the energy is on the celebration of student success, not one harping on the mistakes or failure. As you set goals with your students for SEL, ask yourself if the student has the same conjoint goal, if it is age-appropriate, and if it is possible to measure progress toward the SEL goal. Additionally, how do we celebrate progress versus achievement of SEL goals that are not necessarily as clear-cut when we reach them?

DON'T SET UP A "NO-WIN" SITUATION

Let's suppose for a moment that a student spills a glass of milk across the table at lunch. Now, as the teacher, you ask the child, "Did you spill the milk?" Well, what are the student's choices in this scenario?

1. Admit that I spilled the milk; hence, I will potentially get in trouble for spilling the milk based on what has occurred in mistakes I have made in the past.
2. If I say, "I did not spill the milk," I possibly could get away with it and not get in any trouble.

The second choice might seem like the logical one from the perspective of the student. Why? Because the student has a *100% chance* of getting a consequence with the first response. However, if I state that I did not spill the milk, I may have a chance at not getting into trouble because I defer that I didn't do it.

So how do we handle this issue? If you see a student do something wrong, confront them directly with the infraction. "You took the item when you were not supposed to, and here is your consequence." Do not question what you already know and thereby set the child up for not taking responsibility.

Approach the issue directly without "sugarcoating" or questioning something that you already know the answer to.

THE LOUDER THE VOICE, THE LESS THE RESPONSIBILITY

One certain way for a child not to muster responsibility is for any authority figure to scare them out of taking ownership of their actions. What does this mean? If you have to tell your administrator about an error you made and they are apt to explode on you, do you really want to open that powder keg?

Many of us might say, "You know what? I think I am just going to try to dance around the issue . . . rather than be yelled at or berated." Hence, the situation is avoided from being discussed directly or tabled to a later date (that may never arrive). Meanwhile, the administrator has lulled into a false sense that everything is fine in the social and emotional learning climate because they cannot hear the whispers of the poor educational climate all around them.

ALLOW THE STING OF CONSEQUENCES WHEN RESPONSIBILITY IS NOT TAKEN

Many times, parents try to shield their children from the bitter taste of taking responsibility for their actions. Parents try to step in and tell teachers why their children did not do what they were alleged to have done. These parents may be all too quick to jump and say, "Not my child," and then defend the child from a society that they feel unjustly wronged them. In doing so, defending wrong behavior from their child also stunts them from growing responsibility (and other SEL skills) in a society that necessitates these traits for ultimate success and maturity.

In terms of fostering responsibility, educators must attempt to construct consequences that are "junior" or "miniature" versions of what the student can expect in the so-called *real world* of society. It is important that we do not subject a student to the real world all at once. For instance, one may hear another colleague warn, "In the real world, their behavior would never fly." True, but our goal is to teach students to be "prepared" for that real world and have the classroom be a place of incubation to do so.

HERE ARE JUST A FEW OF THE "REAL" WORLD SEL RULES

1. If a child is mean to other children, those children will not want to be their friend.
2. If you steal or lie, you must confront the person (or persons) that you offended, and it will not be fun.
3. If you procrastinate anything, you will have to make it up at some other time. Likely, that time will be at some period inconvenient to your social life, technology time, or watching your favorite television show(s).
4. If you break it or mess it up, you must fix it or clean it.
5. Treating others the way you want to be treated is important.
6. Treat others the way you want to be treated by them.
7. If you borrow, you must return it in the same condition.
8. If you agree to it, you should complete it.

EDUCATIONAL APPLICATION OF REAL-WORLD RULES

1. Clean up after yourself.
2. If a student procrastinates the completion of work in school, it can be brought home and made to be done at a time that is inconvenient to the student. Think of an adult real-world example: if you are spending time in the faculty room, then you will be grading your papers versus going out to dinner with your friends or seeing that movie. Quite simply, borrowed time is now "owed" and paid at another time inconvenient to you and your schedule.
3. If you borrow something from the library, a friend, or a teacher, it should be given back promptly and in the same condition as it was found. If you do not do so, you lose this privilege of trust to do this for the foreseeable future.
4. If you agree to do a group project or join an organization or a team, you have the responsibility to commit to an equal part of what you are supposed to do. If you do not adhere to your share, then you receive the criticism of both peers and teachers and will be graded respectively.
5. You are responsible for asking questions and clarifying work. It is not the teachers, peers, or parents' responsibility. If you try to shift responsibility, you concurrently must share what you could have done to positively improve the situation.

Are these common-sense rules? Yes. Are they always very commonly used? No. For some students, school may be the only place where they have structure and are held to such accountability. Do not take for granted that a student knows what they are responsible for or how to take on such a role. This framework must be spelled out consistently, and often, as these are the basic tenants that require consistent reinforcement.

DON'T CONFUSE LACK OF RESPONSIBILITY FOR LACK OF ABILITY

Let's suppose that you wanted to be a rock star. If you were encouraged via a great musical contract of several million dollars, have a concert tour that will take you to all the exotic places you have always wanted to go, and you could bring any of your family, all expenses paid, wouldn't you want to do it? Your motivation would be extremely high in this case.

Of course, this wouldn't be a great opportunity, however, if your voice is as scratchy as a wool sweater and your dance moves are as fluid as that of a robot; then you are in serious trouble. It would not matter how much money the contract is worth, nor how much the deal would be sweetened, because if you simply do not have the capabilities to do something, it may just be out of your scope of competence. It is a case of a high level of motivation and a low level of ability for the task at hand.

Often, in the world of education, we can have a parallel issue. Mistakenly, we believe that if we heap large enough rewards, this will energize our students in motivation toward generating positive SEL interactive traits. At times, however, we are presenting a reward that, due to a host of potential obstacles (i.e., physical, emotional, developmental, situational, etc.), a child is simply not capable of acquiring under any circumstances at that time. If we keep pushing, we risk frustration and breaking the will and esteem of the student. We must either tailor a more attainable SEL goal or find a way of addressing the limitation in that particular domain first.

SEL MUST BE MODELED UNDER THE MOST CHALLENGING OF CIRCUMSTANCES

Let's take the scenario of a speeding car; if one gets pulled over, is the police officer going to yell, scream, and belabor the point of their infraction? Or, more likely, are they going to utilize a calm and consistent tone of voice along the lines of "License and registration . . . please"? If you are a yeller as an educator, you will get far less responsibility taking from students due to fear of accepting the consequences of the blame. (See below for more about this.)

Modeling SEL is a simple task when, as educators, we are calm and the stakes are low. Yet, when the stakes become higher, or the educator is tired, frustrated, or overwhelmed, this is precisely when students are looking for the *how* of modeling SEL behaviors. Society does not generally raise its voice and belabor a point of discord with the rule violator. Generally, it is done under a cool calmness with the fewest words or emotional feedback (i.e., when you speed, you are given a ticket and sent on your way; if you don't pay your bill, you get a utility shut-off notice).

DEVELOP AND UNDERSTANDING DEVELOPMENT

If you are a new parent, you quickly realize that both diapers and formula are extremely expensive. Likely, most of these new parents would like to have their child become potty-trained and eat solid foods as soon as possible for the sake of their pocketbooks and sanity. Yet, as motivated as they may be to do this, they also firmly recognize this ability only comes in time with their child's ensuing developmental capabilities.

Likewise, when you ask a student to take responsibility for anything, the initial question to ask yourself is quite simple: Are they capable of doing this at their current developmental stage? See table 2.1 for a quick primer as to what a child is capable of generally being responsible for and when. Be aware that this chart is only a reference for typical development. Children are quite variable, and each meets their milestones in their own time frame accordingly.

DON'T ALWAYS PLAY REF FOR STUDENT DISAGREEMENTS

It is often that students get into minor (non-physical) conflicts and flare-ups with their fellow peers. The first response is to be reactive and jump in and save the day. The issue then becomes that a student may not have an opportunity to develop and learn much-needed assertiveness and other SEL skills if they do not have a chance to spread their wings and master simple conflict-resolution abilities. Instead, what the student may comprehend is that they are simply incapable of asserting themselves and are in need of constant rescuing by adults or peers. These same students have challenges in their ability to take responsibility for their actions as well as emotions and often are the first to finger-point and defer responsibility. They do not use the tools

Table 2.1. Estimated Age and Developmental/Social Skill Levels

ESTIMATED AGE	SOCIAL/DEVELOPMENTAL SKILLS
0–1 Years of Age	Can be soothed by an adult they are familiar with. Will generally accept and be quieted when picked up. Smiles and laughs with positive social interactions. Begins to acknowledge and recognize familiar faces. Can start to display and comprehend basic emotional expressions in a clear manner. May show discomfort when exposed to negative emotions and/or strangers. Shows more comfort around familiar people and anxiety around strangers. Can find ways to soothe him/herself.
2–3 Years of Age	Is able to participate in small groups with other children. Maintains eye contact with others. Is not overly anxious when exploring new situations and can transition from one scenario to another. Likes to play with various toys and objects. Will sit and look at a book. Usually happy and/or able to soothe themselves. Developing an established and reliable sleeping schedule. Expresses sadness when hurt. Will play near (but not always with) peers.
4–5 Years of Age	Comprehend what is positive versus negative behaviors. Begin to have peers that they befriend. Imitate behaviors of adults. Skills of empathy start to evolve. Like to play and utilize imagination skills.
6–8 Years of Age	Understand the concept of playing, sharing, and taking turns with peers. Begin to comprehend different feelings. Start to realize the link of cause and effect/consequences of actions. Can express their feelings in words. Capable of empathizing in correspondence to others. Are able to separate fantasy versus reality. Understand and tell basic humor. Comprehend and utilize imagination.
9–10 Years of Age	Prefer playing with others versus independently. Begin the development of longer-lasting friendships. Become more independent and rule-oriented. Adult and peer approval concern increases. May become increasingly moody/dramatic. Start to recognize their own mood changes and expressions. Grow into a more competitive individual and want to participate in organized competitive activities. Start to understand and take responsibility for actions and behaviors. Can assert a particular point of view and argument.

(*Continued*)

ESTIMATED AGE	SOCIAL/DEVELOPMENTAL SKILLS
11–13 Years of Age	Increasingly more proficient at using assertiveness skills. Care more about peer pressure, material items, clothing, etc. Continue to refine empathy skills. Developing the understanding that there are consequences to their actions. Recognize cause and effect. Better able to handle negative emotions. Ability to be more persistent and develop leadership and community-based skills. Fairness as a "black-and-white" concept. Realize character education traits and values.
14–18 Years of Age	Begin to be aware of what traits are their strengths and weaknesses. Start to distance themselves from their parents. Increasing social circles. Develop some discord and separation from parents and request independence. Friends become more important. Dating begins to become a vital lifestyle element. The ability to make decisions begins to mature.

of conflict-resolution skills necessary for them to carry in times of conflict and disagreement as they believe they are ill-equipped to even try to do so.

In disagreements, the role of the educator should be more of a coach/consultant role to encourage and inoculate them with skills that they may use when a disagreement comes up, such as the following:

- **Finding another student to play with:** Often, students are so engaged in the conflict that they simply forget the option of moving on to another peer who is more agreeable to playing with them at that time.
- **Find another game/activity to do:** When students become so entangled in determining who is right, they develop tunnel vision as to being right versus wrong and winning versus losing. A simple change in scenery/activity can go quite far to de-escalate a conflict.
- **Taking responsibility for one's mistakes:** A true sign of emotional and SEL maturity is the ability to take responsibility for a mistake or some negative consequence. Rehearsing with the student in question what played in causing the conflict is difficult for that pupil to acknowledge. Yet, the ability to recognize their role and develop a sincere apology is a sign of strengthened SEL abilities.
- **No student should have to endure bullying or physical conflict:** It must be noted that there is a major difference between a minor

disagreement and the danger of physical conflict or bullying. Students rely on adults to intervene in these areas, and educators must always do so for the protection of everyone involved immediately.

RESPONSIBILITY BEGINS WITH "U"

Obviously, responsibility is not a social trait fundamental in just students. As we watch television or surf the web, we can see a plethora of adults behaving badly and then denying any credit or responsibility for the carnage left in their wake. Leaders, athletes, actors . . . the list goes on and on of adults who shun taking accountability and point a finger at others.

Similarly, as educators, we are role models and all too human. When we become angered at a situation or the stressors of the unfairness of a particular issue during our day, we may point a finger of responsibility at those around us. Remember, however, our next generation is in earshot and is learning social and emotional skills through what we teach as well as our behavior.

WHAT IS WITHIN THE CHILDHOOD TOOLBOX OF RESPONSIBILITY?

If students are going to learn responsibility, then we must develop the capacity for students to utilize the skills that are necessary to do so. As children, students have only a limited scope of influence and power in society as a whole. However, in preparing them for the world, we must teach them the skills necessary to survive as well as thrive.

A child cannot take responsibility for their actions if they do not know what components are within their scope of abilities to utilize. So let us take a look at what topics we should be teaching children to exercise their capabilities.

Sincere Apologies

When a student has done wrong, they should be obligated to learn and give a sincere apology. This is not the same as the child who makes a "knee-jerk" apology in which they just reflexively apologize for everything that they do. Encouraged apologies, for the mere sake of an apology, are empty and meaningless.

An apology must come with some manner of how to resolve it or a thought of what the student would do differently the next time. Apologies that are done reactively are often made in the heat of emotional reactivity and do nothing to help the student reflect. Rather, give them a few minutes to write or think of a means of restitution against the student(s) they have wronged.

Play Fighting Always Leads to Real Issues

Students developmentally lack full development of the frontal lobe of their brain (the brain's braking system) until age 25. This means that our students' brains are akin to driving a car at full speed without adequate brakes. When they are playing rough at recess or in their interactions, they often lack impulse control, in this instance not leading to real physical conflict. Often, we ask, "What were you thinking?" The answer is they were not, and they were reacting emotionally.

LEARN HOW TO EXPRESS FEELINGS IN AN ASSERTIVE MANNER AND TAKE RESPONSIBILITY FOR YOUR EMOTIONS

- When a child is young and has limited ability to use words and control emotions, they can have a tantrum and leave adults scrambling to play a game of charades trying to find what will appease them. However, as a child becomes older, they should be taught to state what they are feeling, why they feel that way, and how to solve the problem accordingly.
- Often, students equate anger with rage and acting out and, therefore, find it a negative emotion. Students may need reassurance that anger is an acceptable emotion; however, it is not the job of those around the student to guess why they are feeling anger nor predict that they need to remedy the issue. Students who don't learn how to express what they need to resolve anger become adults who don't know how to handle anger. They are the ones who give the "silent treatment," and others are left to guess what is bothering them or what it was that offended them. For all of us, this is an ineffective means of relationship building. Imagine walking into your administrator and trying this strategy.

We must teach our students to be responsible for all of their emotions and actions. Specifically, they are permitted to feel a range of emotions (positive and negative), but doing so requires an expression of them in a useful manner. If a student chooses to express negative emotions or conflicts, they must also simultaneously offer potential solutions for problem resolution.

Students need to learn to take responsibility for themselves in a conflict in an assertive manner. They have to become skilled at how to address an issue without resorting to hitting (aggression) or being a "doormat" (passivity).

Therefore, developing these productive solutions teaches the middle ground of assertive behaviors. As stated earlier, as adults, we must be willing to allow students to experiment with different means of conflict resolution independently. The nature of student relationships tends to have a conflict with a peer one day and being best friends the next moment without adult interference.

KNOW WHAT CHILDREN CAN HANDLE AND WHAT THEY CAN'T (OR SHOULDN'T)

If we spend all of our school days addressing the variety of relatively trivial issues our students encounter, we waste a great deal of our time on empty conflicts. These concerns create an endless cycle of a drama treadmill that impacts the ability to teach class-wide. Therefore, if we are going to teach students responsibility, we must foster a means to organize the hierarchy of responsibilities of the educator and of the student. Let us look at the precarious road that happens if we saddle students with "adult-like" responsibilities.

Students think they want to be handed the role of responsibility because with it comes control, and they think they desire such a desperate lack in the adult-oriented world. Sometimes, we see parents make a cardinal error of allowing children to be exposed to the so-called "adult world" via exposure to issues such as divorce, bills, mortgages, and the like. Doing so creates adult-like anxiety for children who have no means of controlling these issues within the myopic scope of control of youth. This may be a primary reason why we are seeing emotional issues in younger and younger students that were previously reserved for adults.

CLASSROOM ACTIVITY

Wastepaper Basketball

Our students must understand and have a strategy for separation between what is within their control and what should best be deferred into the capable hands of teachers and other adults. Elementary students communicate and work in the world of play primarily, and so when we enter SEL activities in this realm, we reach into their world. Along this vein, it utilizes play in the curriculum to teach what is the role of each party (educator and student) in the various components of responsibility.

Rules

Let us imagine we have two trash cans: one is for the role of teachers and other adults, and the second is for the job of the student. We can now toss items that go into each "can." One can be exclusively those issues that we do not want children to even attempt to take responsibility for handling. These include scenarios such as:

"The Adult Can"

1. Anyone that tells them to keep secrets from their parents (with the exception of surprise parties/gifts, of course).
2. Issues of harassment, intimidation, or bullying.
3. Any time they are "dared" to do anything.
4. Issues in which they, a sibling, or a peer could potentially be hurt.
5. When they are asked to do something or try something that they are not comfortable doing.
6. Any issue that can remotely cause emotional or physical injury.

"The Child Can"

1. Issues of peer conflict (that are not physical or bullying in nature).
2. Work or activities that they should be capable of but have not given themselves a reasonable opportunity to attempt the respective task.
3. Waiting patiently to do something that they are eager to do.

Children Should Toss into the Adult Can

1. Any, and all, matters in which they, or anyone else, has the potential for (or is engaged in) dangerous activities.
2. Scenarios in which anyone suggests keeping something secretive from parents.
3. Concerns in which the student has "butterflies in your stomach" and does not know why.
4. Problems that involve discussions related to harassment, intimidation, or bullying.
5. Suggestions in which a peer/peers try to dare the youth to do something or exert negative peer pressure/influence.
6. Any concern that you are not certain of if you should (or could) handle the topic in an appropriate fashion.

Note: It must be made very clear to students that adults do not want children to handle issues for which students are ill-equipped or not emotionally ready to tackle. Therefore, when topics are adult-oriented or dangerous, they must be deferred to educators quickly and always.

SOME ADDITIONAL THOUGHTS ON RESPONSIBILITY IN SCHOOL

The role of responsibility is never so glaringly clear as that of a student's responsibility within the school setting. For many children, school is the primary means of taking ownership of what they do, experiencing failure or disappointment, and learning to navigate with others who vie for the attention of a teacher, school sports, or clubs.

Therefore, within SEL traits, this responsibility becomes the natural venue in which this topic should be taught and discussed. To foster an environment of responsibility, the following are useful within the public school arena:

1. **Allow for failure**: Allowing for some minor level of failure and disappointment may sometimes be the natural consequence a student needs in order to recognize that they are responsible for their schoolwork and attendance. If they have never experienced failure, they have never learned the tools to remedy it.
2. **Don't belabor mistakes:** When we overly harp on mistakes, students may be less willing to step to the plate and accept their role. Therefore, less discussion and not being overly reactive allow the pupil to feel comfortable coming into the light of acceptance for what they have done.
3. **Encourage positive responsibility**: As humans, we are all tuned to remember the negative more than the positive. As we discussed earlier, it is much easier to recall something negative than the kindest words ever uttered in your presence. Therefore, be certain to celebrate and feed the accomplishments of the students in your class so they bask in the light of positive responsibility.
4. **Responsibility and tasks:** Giving students "chores and tasks" in class and in the school allows them to know that they have a function in the school. In society, adults run and control everything in their lives, and yet school is a student-centered world. We let them know this when they feel a vital member of the educational community.
5. **Have parents involved:** Parents are the greatest model of responsibility for a child. Invite them to participate in school and in their child's learning.

Chapter 3

There Is a Big World Out There
Practical SEL

Play gives children a chance to practice what they are learning.

—Fred Rogers

CHILD PROFILE

Mary is a 12-year-old middle school student. She is enthralled with Legos and anime (Japanese art). Some would say that Mary is obsessed with Legos and art, as that is all she seems to talk about. When she gets older, she hopes to become an anime artist, and she draws her favorite figures obsessively as a means of practicing her hopeful eventual vocation.

Mary also has another goal that she does not always speak of; she wants to have friends desperately. Mary spends hours thinking to herself about anime and projects she can build with her Legos and wants to share those ideas with others. Being an only child does not allow her to talk with peers when she is at home, and she is often shy.

Mary gets her confidence up one day at school and asks her peers if she can spend time with them. She then excitedly tells them about her Lego projects and the various characters that she has memorized in the world of anime. The other girls tell her "Get out of our personal space" and she continues to talk as a few snicker at Mary. Mary bursts into tears, and she walks away with her head hung low in disappointment.

THE REAL WORLD IS FRAUGHT WITH CONFUSING SEL MESSAGES

When one considers it, the world we reside in is fraught with mixed social and emotional messages. Take, for instance, the often-used greeting, "How are you doing today?" We often answer with the words, "Fine, how about you?" It would not matter, generally speaking, if we were having a bad day, a great day, or somewhere in the middle. It is generally expected that we respond with a simple pleasantry back because that is what our society has trained us to do. We would not talk about the fact that we are constipated, have a terrible rash, or that our family situation is in shambles.

Yet, in some other cultures, such as certain Asian cultures, the answer might be a long description of exactly how their day is and the status of these ailments. Or, alternatively, no answer at all because the question you asked was very invasive. In fact, in China, they forego this question and ask the alternative, "Have you eaten?"[1] Similarly, if a student is asked how they are doing today, are they supposed to give an honest answer, or are they supposed to just give the knee-jerk response of "Fine, how about you?"

What of other SEL messages in which we embed sarcasm, humor, or any other conversation nuances that blur the true meaning behind a conversation? The answer would be to make certain as educators that we say what we mean and mean what we say so that we are reaching our students at even the most concrete level. Additionally, if we do utilize an alternate meaning, we should be clear in translating the meaning in a manner the majority of our students understand.

SEL THEORY AND APPLICATION ARE VERY DIFFERENT

If you have ever seen a fast-food commercial, you know that the cheeseburger that they show in the commercial is much different than what you actually receive when you get to the restaurant. The burger depicted in the commercial is clean, neat, and appetizing. Meanwhile, the reality of the burger you get may be anything but that. This is the case with many social-emotional situations we rehearse in class and in counseling: neat and clean social interactions. In reality, they may be anything but clean, neat, and structured. Thus, we must teach students to have the flexibility for a myriad of varying social situations when rehearsing appropriate social interactions.

THE "PLAYER PIANO" MANNER OF "TEACHING" SOCIAL SKILL

As a child, our family had a player piano. We would carefully place the yellowing rolls on the top of the gears. As the rolls spun around, the keys would press down in perfect harmony and sequence as though a ghostly expert pianist had taken a seat at our piano. Oftentimes, we would pretend to play the piano. We became quite proficient at "pretending" to be proverbial virtuosos.

So is the parallel with "teaching" or "learning" SEL. Many of the abilities we try to teach can be "played" back to us in rigid black-and-white tones. Yet, the world of SEL has so many shades of gray that when a student attempts to apply them in a social scenario in school, it comes across as "canned, phony, or inauthentic."[2] Frequently, this lack of genuine interactive style is a turn-off for potential friendships. Students seem to have a keen, tacit knowledge that something seems off or does not ring as true in the interaction and thus back away.

The primary issue with SEL skills is that we use different social and emotional responses depending on the situation, person, or circumstance. For instance, if you have to offer constructive criticism of a colleague, you would take into account the situation, the peer, and the circumstance, almost instantly. Your thought process would immediately recognize that seemingly identical social issues may require different solutions that are dependent on the scenario. This is difficult for a student to understand the subtlety of such actions and why a single solution cannot be used for a parallel social issue.

In the controlled environment that is the classroom, we often don't see how students apply SEL skills because of the priority of teaching the varying curricula. When do we see students establish an understanding (or lack thereof) of SEL attributes? It is at times when adults have the least influence over student interactions, namely, during lunch, recess, study halls, and so on. It is during these times that social and emotional interactions run fast and furious among students.

As the teacher (or school counselor), therefore, those are the times to be "in earshot" to see how students interact. Are they talking about appropriate subjects that are aligned with their peers? Do they allow for back-and-forth dialogue, or do they just dominate the conversation? Do they only talk about themselves, or are they asking open-ended questions? These are the times for educators to listen and perform the role of the SEL life coach, in a sense, offering suggestions and telling them to "get back out there" into that challenging field of peer interaction.

BE AWARE OF MIXED MESSAGES IN SOCIAL INTERACTIONS

When we are teaching social interactions, we must be careful that we develop age-appropriate social skills as a student develops. For instance, especially in the case of special education students, some consider it "cute" to have them hug those that they meet. In fact, it is rare that anyone says anything about this for fear of being mean or discouraging. The problem becomes as they grow older and start to develop vocational skills that the same hugging behavior can be labeled as *inappropriate, uncomfortable*, and, in the far extreme, *harassing*. Think of SEL skills and how they will serve the child now and as they grow into adulthood.

AN INTERESTING CONNECTION BETWEEN READING COMPREHENSION AND EMOTIONAL COMPREHENSION

When we are working with students, we often think of emotional comprehension, emotional intelligence, and reading comprehension as three different categories. Therefore, when we are teaching reading comprehension, we are not necessarily thinking of emotional intelligence or comprehension. Yet, what if those all intersect in some way that makes each of them strengthen the other?

Studies indicate that students with lower reading comprehension also concurrently struggle with the areas of inter and interpersonal capabilities and managing stress.[3] What does this mean for us as educators? Consider that stories and books that highlight human connection, social interactions, and social situations can, in fact, "kill two birds with one stone" in teaching both comprehension emotionally and literacy. Thus, seeking such books serves a twofold purpose.

THE SIX KEYS TO GOOD SEL CURRICULUM

There are an almost infinite number of ways of implementing social-emotional curriculum programs. Some may be more effective and others less effective. So how do we know what are the best ways of developing SEL programs within our individual schools and districts?

Here are six elements that are effective toward a good and systemic SEL program:

- **Immediate:** SEL takes place when you have the most rapid and immediate feedback possible from the other party in the interaction.
- **Real-time:** Often, we practice social interactions; yet providing real-time, actual social interactions that are monitored is the most effective manner of teaching and learning social and emotional learning skills. In school, SEL is "on-the-job" training.
- **Everyone Is an SEL Teacher:** It is not one teacher or counselor that plays the role of an SEL educator. Rather, all those educators that are in the student's life alternate roles between educator, coach, cheerleader, and teacher in helping students navigate varying social interactions and environments throughout the day.
- **Must Be Applied to All Levels of a Student's Lifestyle:** The more places that a student can practice and receive critique at home, school, and work, the better they will be able to apply social-emotional constructs in varying domains of their lifestyle.
- **Include Topics of SEL Relevant to the Student:** Often, we have students read literature because it is "included in a curriculum/program." Thus, they are not motivated to read what is provided to them. Similarly, including topics of social-emotional interactions for the students will foster increased "buy-in" by them when they are conducting social-emotional interactions. These may include such things as social media, making friends, and, later, dating.
- **They Don't Need the Kitchen Sink:** Try to eliminate SEL topics that may be less important in order to prioritize what is vital and what they will need.

THE DANGER OF STARVING SEL SKILLS

In the world of public education, we can feel that we are left with little time but to teach due to ever more demands being placed on the curriculum. That being noted, there is an often unintended side effect for students who do not have frequent opportunities to exercise their SEL muscles. These children tend to find some alternative way to fulfill their social needs but not generally at the most appropriate times during the school day. Namely, they seek to get their social, emotional, and attention needs to be met by negative-attention means.

Let us imagine that you have a student that does not have any play dates, has no siblings, and/or limited social opportunities. They will seek to satisfy the social and emotional cravings at the least appropriate times and junctures because it provides the biggest social and emotional "bang for the buck."[4] For instance, if a child's sole peer outlet is in school, he will utilize this venue to satisfy those needs. It does not matter if you, as the educator, stand on your head if the motivation of the students finds the desire for peer interaction is greater than the drive for learning; they almost always go down that road. In other words, if that particular student believes that the need for socializing is of greater reinforcement to him or her personally, they will seek that every time because it's simply a greater reward. It is not that they do not want the positive reinforcement of your praise; instead, it is that the adulation and laughter with those their own age is simply a greater draw to them. With this in mind, rewards, consequences, or any other motivational tool tried will be moot and inconsequential in this case. The student that is seeking social and emotional attention is like a virtual "kid in a candy store" seeking the reward of any kind of immediate social interaction versus the lower reinforcement of the teacher's verbal praise. It will only take one student to giggle, laugh, or tell them to stop misbehaving to have made some sort of social or emotional connection that they so crave.

SOME STUDENTS ONLY UNDERSTAND THE SEL LANGUAGE OF "ADULT" AND NOT THAT OF CHILDREN

Case in point, regarding social skills, let us suppose a student comes to your school who is an only child. Predominantly, by logic, they are perpetually around adults solely. What they hear is adult talk: adult humor, adult sarcasm, and adult concerns. They only see the predictable ramblings of grown-ups socializing and expressing emotions in, hopefully, mature and predictable ways. In fact, when the child says something at home that sounds grown-up for their age, it is reinforced with a loud parental chuckle and, "Oh . . . isn't that cute?"

Now, picture that the same child arrives at school for their first day among a gaggle of, let's say, kindergarteners. They try to engage with their peers with the learned "adult-like" social-emotional skills. The children simply do not understand this method of conversation as it is foreign to them. Conversely, that student looks at his fellow five-year-olds discussing topics common to five-year-olds and thinks to himself, "Why are these kids acting like a bunch of five-year-olds?" In fact, studies of only-children, and those with siblings significantly older than themselves, show that these children have a higher difficulty in social and mental health acclimation than peers with siblings around their own age when venturing into the school setting.[5] This can continue year after year until the peers' maturity levels reach that of the student's more "adult-like" perceptions and engagement with others.

Oddly, it will take those adults in the child's life to teach the youth how to be able to interact with their peers in an age-appropriate manner. It is as if a child, such as this one, must be taught a language that is native and natural to his peer group. SEL skills can only be taught by being immersed in them and through practice.

FINDING FRIENDSHIPS

There are questions frequently asked as to where a student may find friendships as they become increasingly more challenging to find in the world of social media and organized structured activities. The following are some thoughts in that regard:

- Friends generally are based on location when younger, and interests as children grow older.
- Where has the student found friends in the past?
- Activities are a good manner of developing discipline. Play dates are a good manner of developing social skills for friendship.
- Help children look for peers open to friendship.
- Prune friendships early, if need be, to ensure that children develop quality friendships and avoid those that may be detrimental. As children get older, this becomes increasingly more challenging.
- Teach children to find quality friends and to treat them well no matter which other students they are interacting with.
- Some children prefer a small circle of friends, and that is okay; don't push larger gatherings.
- Introverted children have as many strengths as extroverted children.

THE COMPETENT SEL FLIGHT SIMULATOR

If you were to board a plane and the pilot were to tell you they logged 10,000 hours on a flight simulator but this was their first actual flight, would you trust their skills? The guess would be a resounding no.

Yet, we try a parallel strategy when we tell students to practice "simulated" social and emotional skills solely through interaction with adults (i.e., teachers, therapists, etc.) and then tell them to go out and use these rehearsed skills in the real world. The sole use of this technique is frequently doomed for failure when practice comes to application because it does not look at the nuisances of childhood socialization.

PROVIDE "ON-THE-JOB" SEL TRAINING

If students are going to be socially competent, they must practice this skill like any other comparable exercise. Today's students are drowning in waves of carpools and endless classes from dance to soccer, music to equestrian, and/or karate to ballet. These activities can be helpful in bolstering social and emotional skills, provided they do not create an overwhelming source of anxiety for students and parents alike.

Often, you will hear that these activities are good opportunities for teaching discipline and socialization among students. Despite the vital nature of these organized activities, however, the optimal manner for our students to succeed in socialization is through the practice of being social with their peers. These activities are often highly structured and do not allow for the freedom of dialogue between students that are a hallmark of SEL.

Socializing is like exercising to develop muscles or stamina to run a marathon. One must strengthen their social skills and need to specifically practice, fail, and retune their technique for ultimate success. One cannot learn to run a marathon only by learning the techniques of how to run without actually going through the work of running itself.

Therefore, planned playdates, recess, and lunch all provide the "on-the-job" training in doing so. It is through these groups, or one-to-one, peer interactions that youth can experiment as to what works and what does not when conversing with others. Teachers can give immediate feedback regarding interacting in "real-time" and what is applicable to the situations at hand in these scenarios. These opportunities cannot be replaced by rigidly organized activities that are closely adult-monitored and provide little space for social experimentation.

Often, we, as adults, are too quick to pull a student away from what we see as a potential social failure. However, if we make the analogy to one of a student doing a jigsaw puzzle, we would not pull that same student away when they clumsily try and shuffle pieces back and forth or twist and turn them. We would sit back patiently and wait for that all-important "ah-ha" moment when the puzzle pieces finally fit together. So, too, are social skills. They take time, failure, readjustment, and then eventual success. Think about how many times we have had clumsy social moments in our own lives. It is during these awkward times that we learn the most about ourselves and others.

The suggestion of playdates with compatible peers can offer students a chance to stretch their social prowess. Adults can help guide children on how to handle minor conflicts toward a mutually positive solution. Additionally, monitoring the interactions helping youth to understand peer body language and emotional expression can be established and addressed, as well as how to positively reinforce good social and emotional learning skills.[6] These same objectives can be addressed, to a lesser degree, during recess or free time within the classroom setting.

ALL HANDS ON DECK WITH SEL SKILLS

We have all heard the term, "It takes a village to raise a child."[7] To parallel this analogy, it takes a team approach toward SEL skills in the academic village we call education. Educators must be knit together as a team of coaches for an SEL program or intervention to work. That "coaching team" works together for the benefit of the entire student community. This requires teaching an SEL skill (such as conversation starting) and having the joint buy-in of teachers, counselors, supervisors, and the curriculum for consistency and delivery of this as a school-wide message.

The challenge, as we noted earlier, for students, is that application of SEL skills is not "a simple, one-size-fits-all" approach. When a student is in varying scenarios, the script that they may utilize in one social opportunity may have to completely flip, as it may not be appropriate or useful in another. When a student has only experience of how to apply a single or a limited technique in a social situation, they may try to jam themselves into numerous scenarios using the same imperfect SEL skills that are ineffective or don't quite fit into the new problem. When it fails, if they do not have other tools, they will just try harder with those same SEL skills to make that restrictive skill set work. This only leads to a repetitive cycle of increased resistance by peers and eventual social isolation. As psychologist Abraham Maslow so aptly stated, "If the only tool you have is a hammer, you tend to see every problem as a nail."[8]

It is necessary, therefore, that this child has a crew of adults who are at the ready to help them shift the proverbial gears of their SEL skills for each idiosyncratic situation when the student becomes stuck in the inevitable social mud of life. This must take place with constant, consistent, and prompt reactions during times when social skill education is at its most pivotal.

As educators, we may say, "That is not realistic. Who has time for all of these adults to be involved in one child's day?" A parallel to consider is that the issue of SEL skills is a lot, again, like riding a bike. It only takes a quick redirect and reminder to keep the bike up, balanced, and moving straight ahead (not constant and intensive interventions). Hence, when a student begins to realize that a small supplemental toolbox of SEL skills may help in the majority of social scenarios, they will be, for the most part, set. It does not take but a few moments of social redirection and guidance; less is more, and a quick reminder is often all it takes to get the student back on the social track.

TECHNOLOGY IS THE NEW WORLD OF SEL

Social media is everywhere and is one of the most integral spokes in the social wheel of teaching SEL skills. If a student does not know how to be a digital citizen in society and bridge that with the "brick-and-mortar" world, then there is a very real possibility that they will be left in the dust of many socialization opportunities, both inside and outside the bounds of school.

According to Dr. Carrie Barron, MD, in a 2015 article entitled "How Technical Devices Influence Children's Brains Dangers," she indicates that, "The fast pace of online activity is not only altering the way young people's brains process information, but such activity is also physically changing their brains. The overuse of online activity is reconfiguring children's brains and forcing the field of education to adjust accordingly."[9]

Perhaps, you may not believe that our student's brains are actually being rewired by technology; however, if you are asked, Can you remember the phone numbers of five of your friends? Alternatively, when was the last time you followed someone's directions to a location or read a map (not GPS)? Do you have trouble recalling the phone numbers of your five closest friends; this, too, was a vital survival skill little more than a few years ago. It is now a rarity for anyone to be able to do these basic tasks that previously were a part of most people's regular repertoire.

Without a doubt, technology is (by far) the favorite medium for students to communicate with each other and the world at large. Just watch a group of teenagers walking shoulder to shoulder texting each other with no attempt at actual verbal communication. As a result, any student's SEL skills training must be inclusive of mastery in the domains of social media etiquette, how to handle cyber conflict and cyberbullying, as well as the potential hazards of engaging with individuals who one does not know.

DOES THE STUDENT WANT TO SOCIALIZE?

A difficult reality to sometimes swallow is that all students (and people) exist on a continuum of socialization between introversion and extroversion. Western society falsely holds to a belief that extroverted people are always the best adjusted to the society around them. Conversely, however, many other cultures find introversion as a far more vital attribute than that of Western society (who lean to the converse).

In truth, some students simply prefer independent time and find socializing a draining pursuit if they must constantly interact with peers and engage in the superficial small talk that is punctuated among most in childhood.

Some have a preference for interacting with adults about subjects that are less superficial in nature. Additionally, adults are generally more predictable, have a greater likelihood to listen, and are less likely to argue over seemingly minor triggers. How many times have you seen a teacher arguing with a child over whether they will share the swing at recess?

There is a very decisive attribute toward a student that is more introverted. These students have the leanings toward being more introspective and have a stronger capacity to look at other students' interactions in a more global and systemic manner. These youth harbor an understanding of relationships and how they generally work better than those students that are constantly talkative and socializing. Of course, those that are more reserved should be able to muster the social skills needed at the times that such talents are required for ultimate success in a world that does require competent social interactions. In the world of SEL, it is important that a student knows how to socialize in the world around them. However, extroversion does not need to be the student's primary motivation as they may well feel whole and fulfilled leaning toward a more introverted personality type and should not be pushed away from this perspective.

So how do we know then if an introverted student is in potential need of improved SEL skills specific to conversation and socialization? If they are happy and feel satisfied with the current academic, social, and behavioral aspects of their lives and it is not an obstacle to others, what is the harm of allowing them to remain in this level of comfort? Further, if no major obstacles to social skills do not adversely affect their behavior, health, academics, vocation, or the rights of others, then it may not need to come to the immediate forefront of concern. The attribute of introversion has a dynamic interplay of personality, culture, and socialization that we must not compare with our own level of comfort in these areas. Culturally, in places like Japan, Finland, Sweden, and Switzerland, introversion is considered a strength, and children and adults are valued for their quiet and contemplative personalities.[10] Thus, it is important that we look for a cultural aspect to a student's personality makeup.

UNDERSTANDING SOCIAL ANXIETY AND SEL

True social anxiety in children is not an uncommon occurrence and can act as an obstacle to a student developing and utilizing the necessary SEL skills. In teens, the prevalence of social anxiety is 11.2% for females and 7% for males.[11] Therefore, it is important to think of some traits of anxiety in socializing when considering SEL in students.

- **The More You Avoid the Obstacles, the Larger and More Foreboding They Become:** Sometimes well-meaning adults try to keep students from having to face their fears. What this creates, in fact, is the opposite effect of validating that their imagined fears are real, and they grow larger.
- **As You Get Closer to the Mountain of Fear, It Gets Bigger:** When students get closer to the items that create anxiety, the fear will grow (and so will the behaviors) until they "get over the proverbial hump," at which time the anxiety will dramatically lessen.
- **What They See Is Different Than What Others See:** A student's perception of fear and anxiety may be irrational or completely different than what others may view it as. The more you understand the anxiety from the student's perspective, the better.
- **Look for Friends That May Climb the Mountain With Them:** Students tend to have less anxiety when they have other peers that they trust and believe in with them in the journey.
- **You Have to Plan the Climb Ahead of Time:** The more a student knows on the front end of a particular transition or anxiety-provoking situation, the more control and less anxiety they will have as they are actually going through it.

NOT ALL STUDENTS CONSIDER "PLAY" TO BE THE SAME ACTIVITY

We often assume that socialization is equated with that activity. If a student is outside on the playground, they should be physically active as their preferred means of activity. As obesity levels have risen to astronomical degrees, there is no doubt that appropriate exercise is a vital and necessary activity.

Unfortunately, play and socialization are not such simple concepts. Some children prefer being engaged in more introspective activities such as reading or playing a board game. Forcing them to engage in activities far outside their social comfort zone pushes the issue of socializing as well as engaging in activities that they do not inherently want to do. Additionally, it has the side impact of making them feel that they must be extroverted to be fully accepted. Again, this is not downplaying the importance of physical activity. It is just to realize that the stereotype of "students constantly running around playing" is not the inherent pastime that all children gravitate toward.

FIND SIMILAR INTERESTS

According to relational psychology, two of the best means of building a budding friendship are proximity (how close and often one person is to another) and similar interests (hobbies, subjects, etc.). Those that tend to have issues with social skill deficits have two issues against them: they tend to be hesitant to socialize, and they may have interests that are outside the norm of their peers.

Therefore, to feed a potential successful friendship is to place a child in close proximity to a peer(s) who has/have similar interests. This will likely plant the relationship in the most fertile soil for a friendship to potentially bloom.

It is, in this case, that the following are necessary elements for the potentially successful incubation of social interaction success:

- Organized activity that allows time for free socialization (such as recess, free time, lunch)
- Interaction that is based on the specific and mutually shared interests of those involved (sports, Legos, etc.)
- Proximity of peers to each other to facilitate social activity outside the organized activity (close in proximity via class, neighborhood, and organized activities)
- Parental involvement to organize dates and times for the children to get together as a follow-up to the organized activity

Of course, the converse is true. If you want a student to not have a relationship with another student who is a potential bad influence; significantly limit the time and contact they have, and you will prune that relationship from your student's social tree.

Sometimes students will "psych" themselves out before they even initiate the process of socializing. It is far easier to not try than risk the pain and disappointment of outright failure.

Watch for these self-defeating "brain bullies" that counter obstacles to friendships:

- **"All-or-Nothing" Thinking:** These are students that think that every social encounter must result in a best friend forever (BFF), or they feel they have totally failed at socializing. In reality, social skills are not an either/or proposition. Due to the concrete nature and lack of abstract thinking, however, some students think either they have to be the greatest of friends or they are not truly friends with others. In reality, we all

have relationships across a spectrum, from strangers to an acquaintance to that of a friend. The harsh reality to be learned is you cannot be friends with everyone; nor will each student you meet want to befriend you.
- **"Not Seeing the Gray Areas"**: Socializing is, again, a gray-area activity. That is, it is rarely something that can be defined by the simple constructs of "right" or "wrong." This is difficult for students who are very concrete (especially special education students and/or younger students). These students seek to find a black-or-white concrete response to most issues. Socializing operates primarily in shades of gray. Therefore, we must help students to see the gray shades between what they believe to be "right or wrong," "fair or unfair," and "good or bad," as socializing operates primarily in those ambiguous regions.

Let's take a prime example of this mode of student thinking that occurs in the school setting. Students will point out to a substitute teacher the "correct way" their regular teacher does things. They see their teacher's routine as the right and only means possible. It does not occur to them that there are an invariable number of alternate means of conducting a class.

Therefore, as adults, it is important that we show them a number of alternate ways to look at the same experience. In short, this means assisting them to see that socialization is not an "either/or" situation but something that can be addressed in any number of possible ways. It is through brainstorming with an adult that they can develop and garner new methods.

- **Not Every Social Situation (Nor Person) Is the Same:** Some students are more persistent in attempting to socialize, while other students are more apt to give up quickly and limp away in defeat. A student can only use the skills that they have to interact with their peers. Those students may use these limited skills and try one or two attempts at socializing and then determine that "everyone" or "no one" will accept their means of socializing. In short, encouraging a student to not generalize one or two situations to an entire life skill is of vital importance as they are basing a broad response on very limited information. Rather, we have to provide more tools in their toolbox aside from the one or two within their SEL "comfort zone" that they cling close to.
- **When a Student Is Wrong:** Students, like adults, sometimes make assumptions based on little, or false, evidence about an actual situation. For instance, let us suppose that a student sees a peer walking down the hallway and greets them with a simple but barely audible "hello." The peer that they attempted to engage with walks by them without any acknowledgment of their greeting.
  - The student who evoked the greeting may now surmise the following:

- "I said something that hurt their feelings."
- "They don't like me, and so they ignored me."
- "They hate me!"
- "They are rude, and I am never talking to them again."
- There are, however, of course, several alternative logical means of looking at this situation that the student may tend to overlook. Yet, the alternatives that this student may neglect to think of are just as viable and are far less devastating and disruptive to their socialization.

For instance:

- "Perhaps, they did not hear me."
- "Maybe they have headphones in their ears and couldn't hear."
- "Maybe they were thinking about something else."
- "Maybe I spoke too quietly, or it was too loud in the hallway for them to hear me."

It is in these ways that the student starts arguing with the internal dialogue in their head; the more they do so, the more it discourages them from believing in their social skills and abilities. Thus, such dialogue degrades their self-confidence and esteem further.

"IT IS NOT ALL ABOUT THEM"

Students (and even most adults) tend to see most situations that occur from, "What is/was my role in this outcome or in its initiation?" From that perspective, they ask questions such as, "Why did they do this to me?" This internal conversation then leads down a long road of feeling sorry for oneself and believing that you are a perpetual victim. In reality, many social issues do not occur because someone sought *to do* something to the child; rather, it was because they were simply *not thought* of by the other child, who was also in their own egocentric realm in their own right. Coming up with alternative theories for a peer's behavior allows students to think of another theory outside their own narrow beliefs of self-centered motivations and fears.

BLAMING OTHERS DOES NOT HELP YOURSELF

Many children inadvertently associate mistakes with punishment or shame. Hence, they potentially shift the blame from themselves to elevate such pain. In other words, it is simply easier to cushion our own fragile ego by saying that we did not do or are not responsible for something. Students tend to blame peers for not socializing or, alternatively, they will skew a situation so it makes them appear to be the victim. As a direct consequence, they can establish having "no fault" for a relationship or situation not working out in the social arena, which is safer for them emotionally. This strategy, in the short term, may work because it limits the student's feelings of guilt and blame. Along those lines, however, it suspends the student's own inherent ability to take responsibility for their actions, dissect the communications, and observe what they might have done differently.

Let's take a look at an alternative example: Suppose a parent is making a child dinner and starts with the innocuous question, "What do you want for dinner?" The parent goes through the long litany of "What do you want to eat?" and proceeds with a list of potential foods. The child then tells the parent, "I don't want this or that," and then blames the parent for making the wrong meal and for causing them to be disappointed. The child falsely believes that telling someone what you *do not* want is productive communication for telling what *you do* want or need and that when others can't essentially "read your mind," it is their fault. Students must learn that emotional regulation and changes come from learning and trying versus blaming others for what went wrong or what they did. In short, social skills develop from first recognizing the need to change and then doing so.

TOO CLOSE FOR COMFORT

When our students are in preschool and kindergarten, they may not have a good awareness of the personal space around them. When they sit on the carpet or gather in groups, they tend to bang together like a rack of pool balls. However, this tends to create hostility among the other students who associate accidental physical contact with aggression. Alternatively, it is frustrating and confusing for the student who is unaware of physical boundaries and does not understand the reaction that they receive due to a lack of spatial awareness. It is also important to keep in mind that spatial awareness has a cultural component, with certain cultures having different acceptable levels of spatial awareness.

Role-playing for students on an asphalt section of the playground can be useful: draw concentric circles in chalk (with your child in the middle) and discuss who should be in which circle(s) (i.e., defining strangers, family, friends, acquaintances, and self). Review when an imagined peer is too close to you or someone else and how that may make the other person feel. This type of direct criticism and suggestion is necessary for the student to understand consistently and immediately their effect on others. That being said, when peers do not say anything about this behavior, it simply does not provide the much-needed information in a timely fashion for this skill to be learned.

THE GAMES KIDS PLAY

Student games have rules. We are not talking about the specific, concrete rules for a game like tag. Rather, we are talking about the subtle and tacit guidelines that children follow as their own social society outside of the purview of teachers and other adults. Children that do not learn the lesson of proximity grow into adults who are perpetually close-talkers and have little awareness of the discomfort this causes some.

Rule 1: Games Have a Natural Starting and Ending Point

Typically, if students are in the middle of a game or activity, they must finish this game to its natural conclusion before they will allow another peer(s) into the group. This means that if a student attempts to "jam" him or herself into an activity in the middle or at the wrong time, they are more than likely to be rejected. One can see a similar reaction if a parent "pulls the plug" on a video game in the middle of gameplay. The child has little tolerance for an abrupt transition and closure of the activity.

A student with lessened social skill abilities may not be aware of the starting and ending of activities among their peers. With few SEL skills in their toolbox, they try the few they have with more force and vigor. This is the equivalent of "banging their head" against the proverbial wall as they try to enter the respective activity within their peer's social circles without much success. This perceived failure thus decreases their self-esteem because they believe their peer group as a whole is rejecting them. In the tunnel vision of anger and sadness, most students with lower SEL skills never even think of any alternative coping strategy, such as seeking out other peers or activities outside of that immediate peer circle unless it is specifically pointed out to them by teachers (or sometimes other peers).

Rule 2: Look for the Wallflowers

Teaching the student to scan the environment when initially rejected by the first peer group for acceptance by another will greatly increase the likelihood that the second group of students will welcome them. Coaching the student to practice assessing when a social activity has reached its natural conclusion and then trying to join a group is immensely useful. This can be helpful as they grow at a playground, dance, or other peer/social event.

Rule 3: Teaching Your Student a "Pickup" Line for Conversation Is Vital

Now, the suggestion is not a cheesy line that would be used in a 1970s dating video. Rather, what it meant is we all have statements and questions that we use to engage acquaintances around us. Some students have one or two opening conversation starters, and if they don't elicit a response that creates dialogue, they do not have the necessary SEL traits to interact with peers.

Teaching the student to ask a question, give a compliment, or state something they have in common is the first step to developing deeper conversations. In short, the more open-ended questions a child has in a rehearsed script in their back pocket, the better. The more questions and the fewer statements made, the better.

Open-Ended Questions Students Can Use

- What is your favorite video game? Why?
- What is your favorite board game? Why?
- How do you do that (whatever activity)? Can you help me to do that?
- Whom do you play with? Can I play? What are the rules for playing this game?
- What is the homework? Do you find it easy or hard?

Rule 4: A Novel Skill or Item Can Be a Novel Way of Drawing Others

If a student has some item or novel skill that his or her peers do not have that can out other children's natural curiosity, this can often be an unusual icebreaker yet very effective.

Examples of this include the following:

- An unusual ability, such as being proficient in drawing
- Learning and being able to do a magic trick in front of a crowd of peers
- Having a new idea for a game that others have not played

These opportunities generate inquisitiveness among the student's peer group, and children from far and wide are drawn as child-like moths to a flame. Generating a quick flurry of interest and popularity can be utilized to garner and then harness friendships.

Rule 5: Most Other Kids Stay Away From "The Know-It-All," "Boss," or "Rule-Keeper"

Students with SEL challenges sometimes will attempt to overcompensate for these deficits by acting as a know-it-all or being overly bossy, a rule-keeper, or a tattletale. If we prune these tendencies as the child begins to feel more comfortable and try to focus on securing a place in the social and conversational arena, these behaviors dwindle. Still, it is vital to be on the lookout for these behaviors and squelch them as soon as you can, as they can grow into a habit and socialization obstacle that leads to further rejection/isolation.

EDUCATIONAL APPLICATION

Generally, school is the one place where youth of society all congregate together. A slice of each respective community represents the socioeconomic, cultural, and racial makeup of every faction of a town. This makes it the best petri dish from which our pupils can formulate the necessary SEL skills to build the scaffolding necessary for adult life.

To develop a good social skills program within a school system, we must consider the following:

- **Be Where You Are Needed Most:** The times that SEL skills are most tested and the student's SEL abilities are most needed occur where teachers are least present: lunch, recess, dances, school-sanctioned activities, locker rooms, and bathrooms. Obviously, we cannot be in some of these locations (bathrooms and locker rooms); however, where we can be present is where we need to listen in earshot and coach our students along to make good decisions socially. These do not need to be long, drawn-out lessons but, instead, a quick and practical statement of SEL advice is all that it may take.
- **Encourage Organized Activities and Team Building Among All Stakeholders:** The first necessary component for socialization is knowing the time to do so. Organized activities and team-building allow students to work together toward common philanthropic or other goals. It should be noted that this occurs "from the top down" so a school faculty that works as a team models a pupil community to do so as well. If school climate and teamwork are not evident, the students will learn more by behavior than by empty words.
- **Role Modeling Social Skills Within the Classrooms:** It should not be assumed that all students know and can employ SEL skills. Think, again, of the child that was an only child and solely interacted with

adults. When they arrive in school, how are they supposed to learn how to interact with those 20 years younger than anyone that they talked with previously? Lessons should include from the outset of each school year socialization, greetings, and conflict-resolution skills.

- **Encourage Problem-Solving:** Especially young children like to involve the teacher in minor squabbles and issues. Encourage them to take care of minor issues and offer potential solutions that will foster the negotiation skills necessary for a child to thrive and prosper. Additionally, it will avoid the social isolation that comes from squealing on those that you wish to befriend.
- **Raising Your Hand Is a Social Skill:** Have you ever met people that talk over you or don't let you get a word in edgewise? When a student blurts out an answer, that is the junior equivalent. Therefore, stress that one must wait to be called on, and if the pupil has trouble remembering this, encourage that they have to put their finger on their lips (while raising their alternate hand) to keep themselves quiet every time they raise their hand, which can assist in this manner.
- **Being Kind:** The most vital rule may also be the simplest. Be kind in the words you say, with your hands as well as your feet, and follow the "golden rule." If this is touted often and always, as well as trying to be, "the best me that they can be" versus competing, this can go a long way toward practical social skills.

Chapter 4

A Walk in Someone Else's Shoes . . .

Helping Students to Develop Compassion and Empathy

Empathy grows as we learn.

—Alice Miller

CHILD PROFILE

Luis is a 12-year-old who is in a class at his local public middle school. Luis often is a "know-it-all" and sticks his nose into everyone else's business offering unasked-for advice and opinions. He is sometimes labeled a "bully" because he often tells others he simply "does not care what anyone else thinks."

He has been known to "enjoy" making others cry by embarrassing or laughing at them. He is the first to spread a rumor or tease a fellow student if it means that his name will also circulate around the daily gossip of the school. He states that he does not care if his popularity is at the expense of others; he simply thinks the attention is attention (good, bad, or indifferent).

WHY IS EMPATHY SUCH A DIFFICULT SKILL FOR STUDENTS?

We often hear the phrase, "Kids can be cruel." That is a time-tested mantra that is often uttered by adults in relation to how children treat each other. If you can remember as a child being picked last or being teased or bullied, you may be quick to confirm that this is indeed true.

Children, by nature, are blatantly honest, curious, and exhibit constant learning by trial and error.[1] When they are young, they are taught (hopefully) not to lie. These children often will give the unvarnished, unfiltered truth of how they see things. If the person beside them is overweight, they might say they are "fat"; if they see someone with a physical disability, they may be quick to point out the obvious and question it loudly.[2] They are devoid of "political correctness" or insight.

This means they must be taught how to address the subject of honesty tempered with tact. We can teach our students that tactful honesty means stating how they feel directly without hurting another peer's feelings. When criticism of another is involved, it also means avoiding harmful labels such as "jerk" or "bully." Rather, this means voicing the specific behavior in question and what actions they wish for the peer to cease doing. If a student is to make a comment that may be perceived as criticism, help them to couch the statement with a primary positive comment of the peer and conclude it with another positive statement (much like a sandwich).[3]

For instance:

- When questioning about a characteristic of someone else, this should be done using an "inside voice," and questions should be directed to the parent or other authority figure quietly versus the person in question.
- Before making a statement about someone else, first put your finger on your lips (a physical reminder) and ask yourself, "How would I feel if this was said about me?" This serves as a consistent reminder of the old adage, "If you don't have something nice to say, don't say it."
- Model tact yourself; if you are someone that uses direct communication to the point of coming across as aggressive, then you must begin to show your child how to tactfully deal with interactions with others in an assertive versus aggressive fashion. Remember, children learn infinitely more from what we do than from what we say.

THE EGOCENTRIC NATURE OF CHILDREN

Children tend to be egocentric; that is, they see the moon, the stars, and everyone orbiting in their lives as revolving around their tiny egos.[4] When they are young, they have difficulty understanding the concept of empathy and the possibility of other points of view. It takes burgeoning maturity and reminding via adults to demonstrate this complex life skill for them to understand that there are other viewpoints and ways of thinking aside from their own.

This is why the skill of empathy is a crucial and necessary ability to be taught. As a child, the idea of being able to see outside of oneself is counterintuitive. After all, if you are the apple of your parent's eye, shouldn't everyone feel similarly about you? Yet, it is those children capable of the ability to grow in empathy and compassionate development early that reap the incredible benefits versus those who are delayed in fostering these skills.

EMPATHY IS BECOMING EXTINCT

Study after study suggests that empathy is becoming ever shorter in supply. Children are becoming more egocentric and less empathetic in their relationships with peers and adults.

For instance:

- A study published in 2011 in the *Journal of Personality and Social Psychology Review* found a "decline of 48 percent in college students' scores on empathic concern, a measure of feelings of sympathy, tenderness, and compassion for others. There was also a parallel 34 percent decline in perspective-taking (to) imagine another's point of view."[5]
- Sara Konrath and her colleagues took advantage of this wealth of data by collating self-reported empathy scores of nearly 14,000 students. She then used a technique known as cross-temporal meta-analysis to measure whether scores have varied over the years. The results were startling: Almost 75% of students today rate themselves as less empathic than the average student 30 years ago.[6]

SO WHAT DO WE DO?

The statistics show a definite and important correlation between empathy and success. Conversely, some studies seem to show empathy on the decline.[7] So, the question then becomes how do we inoculate our children from this onslaught of decreasing empathy and improve their futures in developing lasting and meaningful social skills and relationships? Empathy cannot be a technique utilized but an environment created that surrounds our students.

THE "SELFIE" SOCIETY

A relatively recent phenomenon has become the "selfie." The "selfie" has become the virtual self-portrait of the new generation. Look around, and you will see teenagers smiling, posing, and twisting in all types of positions to model in their own photo shoots. It may be a tropical destination, with a celebrity, or just to say, "Hey, I am here." It seems innocuous, but in reality, it is the opposite of empathetic behavior; after all, it is called a "selfie," not an "unselfie."

When you are taking a "selfie," you are unlikely to notice others or their emotions.[8] As one stares into the camera of their smartphone, they tend to tune out those around them. Also, children who see the selfies of others tend to think that their lives or daily activities are not as glamorous as those of their peers who manufacture their image through the lens of a smartphone and in the form of social media.

The warm glow of the smartphone is akin to a moth to a flame for upcoming generations. Simply, looking up and looking out toward peers goes a long way to putting their finger on the pulse of those around them.

TEACH CHILDREN HOW GOOD THEY HAVE IT

The mission statement for parenting at its bare bones, in reality, is quite simple. Provide a child with a roof over their head, food on the table, clothing on their backs, and love to fill their heart. Yet, children have taken this a step further to mean a smartphone in their hand, a flat-screen television in their room, and the best brand-name clothes on their backs.

As a result of this competitive nature to have more and more as adults, we have competitively responded to this by giving more and more. It has become an expectation to have materialistic items for both children and parents alike. One does not want to be left out in the cold with a non-brand-name item and risk the scorn of their peers.

It will not occur to a child to be empathetic if they only are able to see the small world of seeking the latest item(s) and if they do not realize that others do not have these things. As adults, we seek to support the learning of our children in public education. Sometimes, however, in all the extracurricular activities and school events, we forget that an element just as important is to support the expansion of their vision to understanding how others live and compassion for those who struggle in our communities. This means teaching our children service to others. This can be accomplished by the following:

- Taking your children to places in which they can provide community service to others that are less fortunate than they are, such as a food bank.
- Encouraging their participation in activities that provide organized philanthropic activities, such as Boy Scouts or Girl Scouts.
- Having them sacrifice something that is important to them to another child or organization to develop the idea of sharing with others who are less fortunate.
- Model for your children using empathy through watching you serve others and making it a point to discuss this with them accordingly.
- Use social media and television as an opportunity to open a dialogue to their opinion and thoughts on stories of others that have less than they do and encourage them to be in touch with their emotions in regard to this.
- When a child has an idea to give or help others (provided it is safe and within your discretion), support them.
- Teach children service to their families through chores. Chores are a means of learning how to help others and demonstrate that they are a valued, necessary, and important member of the family "team."

YOU ARE NEVER TOO YOUNG TO VOLUNTEER

It is typical for children to live in a "me" society—"What is in it for me?" This is compounded by the fact that children are initially noted to have thoughts (as we have discussed) associated with the belief that everything that goes on in their world is somehow personalized to something they did, or did not do. Parenting styles, likewise, have also transformed in which we tend to hover over our children.[9] This can lend itself to stifling the ability for a child to look outside one's self.

There is a very real danger associated with children who continue to seek or believe that the world revolves around them. As they enter the environment of the school in which peers also seek the teacher's limited attention, they become angry and jealous. Sometimes these same children seek to "cut to the chase" and utilize negative attentional behaviors as the easiest means and getting "the biggest bang for the buck" by using these maladaptive behaviors.

Volunteering gives children a sense of control and purpose. Think about it. Adults control each and every aspect of their existence: when/what they eat, what they wear, when they wake up, and even when they go to the bathroom. Children are perpetual "one down" in that they are always cared for. The saying, "Children should be seen and not heard," is a common enough saying. It points to a very crucial aspect of a child's life; however, what is the purpose if everyone is always taking care of me?

Volunteering turns the tables on that a bit. Now a child has an opportunity to "level the playing field" a bit as they have a voice (even if it is albeit small) in the world that they will one day inherit. Children are motivated, often, by the ability to have control, and helping in their community through volunteering creates an amplified impact for both.

The following are some ideas for a child that will allow them the chance to have some role in the world and, in turn, opportunities for confidence building. Keep in mind that safety is paramount in any activity, and so, as a parent or educator, exercising good judgment and volunteering alongside a child is always the best strategy:

- **Consider visiting a nursing home:** Elderly persons often crave the vitality and energy of youth. Many nursing homes have an activity director that can provide a list of scheduled activities that you and your child can join or assist with. Doing so teaches your child that the elderly are persons of wisdom, deserving of respect, and can teach a lot about a previous generation. Additionally, it teaches children about the cycle of life and allows them to discuss first-hand some life lessons (if age-appropriate in nature).
- **Help at a local food pantry:** Our children often take the most basic items for granted: food, shelter, and clothing. Yet, the most basic of items are the most vital for us all. An eye-opening experience is to take them to donate food directly to a food pantry and explain the purpose of these important social service resources.
- **Go to the library:** The library is a wonderful place to blend a love of reading with activities. Offering to help in a library is a win-win situation for all as you are instilling community with the joy of books. One can also seek books that discuss ideas surrounding socializing and emotional regulation to further bolster ideas surrounding SEL.
- **Local scouting opportunities:** Scouting provides an organized opportunity for your child to develop a sense of philanthropy and leadership among their peers. These organizations often require in their activities volunteer requirements.
- **Religious activities:** Religious-based charitable activities often tie nicely into meeting the spiritual, charitable, and empathetic needs of a child and can be done in the context of a family.
- **Thank you notes, pictures, and cards go a long way:** Having your child draw pictures, notes, or cards to people in the hospital, troops far

away, or those that are not able to get out of their homes is a wonderful way to put their artistic and empathetic talents to good use.
- **Have your children see you volunteer:** If you do not volunteer, your child will not see the purpose of doing so within the paradigm of their own life. Explain to them the importance of "giving back."

TO BE EMPATHETIC AND COMPASSIONATE, YOU MUST FIRST UNDERSTAND FEELINGS

Each child varies in their emotional aptitude, or what Daniel Goleman has coined Emotional Intelligence (EQ or EI). EQ is a term created by two researchers—Peter Salavoy and John Mayer—and popularized by Goleman in his 1996 book of the same name. EQ is defined as the ability to recognize, understand, and manage our own emotions.[10]

In a 2013 article in *Forbes* magazine, they found that a research study by the Carnegie Institute of Technology concluded that 85% of financial achievement is due to skills like your personality and your ability to communicate and demonstrate leadership (EQ skills).[11] This, versus the common IQ skills, which only 15% are deemed "technical knowledge."[12] In other words, to establish true success requires EQ versus the previously touted IQ.

BUILDING THE EMOTIONAL INTELLIGENCE OF A CHILD

Making your child more aware of their emotions and the complexity of these feelings can help build EQ/EI. Additionally, sharing with your child your own emotions and why you feel the way you do can help in also enhancing their own ability to read the emotional atmosphere that surrounds them. Finally, even something as simple as watching television and questioning the "mood/emotion" of each character can draw EQ/EI, even in recreational moments.

This will also help your child when feelings seem to "come out of the blue." For instance, when the youth become sad and angry, yet they cannot seem to identify what it is that is bothering them. By discussing and practicing studying their feelings about themselves and others, they can more readily identify what is going on for them. They will also begin to recognize the combination of feelings, such as mad + sad = frustration, excited + nervous = anxious, and so on.

HELP THE CHILD TO REALIZE WHEN THEY ARE GOING DOWN THE WRONG EMOTIONAL PATH

Be honest; when they have said something inappropriate to the situation or made a joke that is not in the correct context, it is vital that they receive immediate feedback. If your child does not get that rapid feedback, they are likely to carry on down the road of inappropriate or insensitive comments. Swift response means rapid return back to a more appropriate social pathway.

ASK QUESTIONS

While we will discuss the formation of asking questions for communication skills later in this book, the idea of simply being open to ask questions of others is a key to developing empathy. Often, younger children especially mistake questions for statements. So when told to ask a question (or if they have a question), they will simply make a statement or tell a story. Formulation of open-ended questions is a key to getting youth to be able to understand and draw into another peer's world.

EDUCATIONAL APPLICATION

Some of our students live in worlds that we cannot imagine. Right outside the doors of every school (yes, including yours) are issues in which families are struggling to put food on the table, families that have no water or power, and/or families dealing with domestic violence as well as abuse and neglect. When we go home at night, these are the children that make us toss and turn to wonder what they are going through and if they are going to be sitting at their desks tomorrow.

Our children live in isolated worlds. Some of them are exposed to more than we can imagine; others are not exposed to anything at all due to being overly protected. Yet, we want them to have some degree of realization of what their fellow children may be going through, even a small bit, so that they can develop the oh-so-vital humanistic trait of empathy. It is only through being in one's shoes that we can feel the pebbles that they walk with on a daily basis.

WHILE DEVELOPING THE TRAIT OF EMPATHY INTO YOUR CURRICULAR PROGRAMMING IN YOUR SCHOOL, KEEP IN MIND THE FOLLOWING

- **Seek Reading and Stories of Those That Have Overcome Adversity:** Helping a child to understand adversity and troubles that others have triumphed over allows them to feel for that person (real or fictional).
- **Encourage Philanthropic Organizations Involvement:** In our communities, there are a great number of civic organizations doing amazing things for those less fortunate. Teaming with them and having them share these stories when appropriate gives our pupils a more open perspective of the world that is outside their own.
- **Model Empathy:** Many times, the problems and issues that students are experiencing seem less vital or catastrophic than those of adults. Therefore, as adults, we minimize or downplay them. Encouraging students to share their stories and modeling understanding and empathy carries things a long way.
- **Celebrate Empathy:** When you see students who gather around a crying peer and offer to help and support them, this is worthy of praise and celebration. Consider praising these "events" individually, in a small group, with assemblies, or all three. Empathy is a trait that is so often pushed to the back burner in the heat of a competitive world.

Chapter 5

What Is With All This Mindfulness?

The way you speak to yourself matters.

—Unknown

CHILD PROFILE

Mohammed is a 12-year-old student who is in an Advanced Algebra class and puts a great deal of pressure on himself academically. As he prepares for his math test, he breaks into a cold sweat and feels his hands begin to moisten with perspiration. He can feel his heart beating out of his chest, and the sweaty hands make his pencil slip from his grip. Mohammed begins breathing rapidly as thoughts of failure and lack of preparation swarm his mind. He tries to swat them away, but they return like mosquitoes on a hot summer day. A million thoughts flood his mind, and the harder he tries to get ahold of and focus, the more his thoughts slip from his grasp like a lathered bar of soap. He is struggling but falling into the quicksand of his own thoughts.

WHY MINDFULNESS?

Mindfulness is essentially an oxymoron because the goal is to empty the mind of thought and focus on oneself. By the age of two, 92% of American children have some sort of presence online. A survey in 2011 indicated that we take in five times as much information daily than we did in 1986. Put another way, it is like reading, or being exposed to, 174 newspapers and processing 34 gigabytes of data each day.[1] This requires children to proverbially drink information from the stream of a firehose of data. Is it any wonder that our children have short attention spans when so much information is flooding and overloading their brains on a daily basis? With so much information, it is necessary to empty a full mind to decrease anxiety and allow one's mind time away from the constant information stream and overload.

WHAT REALLY IS MINDFULNESS?

Mindfulness, in the simplest of definitions, is being able to slow oneself down and focus and pay attention to something fully.[2] This is not an easy skill when information is thrown at our students at ever faster clips by society (much of which is not appropriate for their age). Trying to discern and prioritize information for our youth is like trying to play a never-ending game of Tetris in which the stream of information is relentless, seemingly infinite, and difficult to fit into their young lives. With over six million students (9.4% of the population) having a diagnosis of attention deficit disorder (ADD), the inability to focus has reached near epidemic proportions.[3]

According to social psychologist Dr. Daniel Goleman, students have ever more distractions than in any generation previous. That being said, teaching students to develop mindfulness and increase their ability to focus and help drown out distractions is even more vital.[4] In doing so, this aptitude to foster discipline and focus one's thought process is determined to be an even higher predictor of monetary success than IQ or even inheritance of financial successes.[5]

Further supporting this train of thought, earlier in this book, we referenced a similar study in which children who could hold off and wait for two marshmallows versus taking a single one immediately were found to have the emotional discipline to succeed throughout their lifetime. Hence the ability to maintain focus and patience is key if we are going to prepare students, not just in academic skills but also life skills as ever more distractions tug for their attention.

Parents often say, "What about my child who plays video games for hours on end in a trance of almost seemingly infinite focus?" Many of these games require short stents of focus by looking at characters and objects in varying places on a screen. Therefore, it requires minute snippets of focus versus intense concentration on a particular subject. This is a strength of students with attention issues (who focus on everything at once) and our new generation of technologically wired youth.[6]

MINDFULNESS VERSUS SEL

Though we often discuss mindfulness and SEL in the same breath, they are, in reality, two different concepts that often seek to produce comparable results in teaching youth how to recognize their emotions and interact with others along this vein. Mindfulness is more of an individually based paradigm, and SEL is more of a broad goal in the larger context of society and socialization in the world at large.[7] As Linda Lantieri and Vicki Zakrzewski, two veteran educators, so succinctly indicated, SEL is an outside-in approach, and mindfulness is the opposite in its application.[8]

THE DEVIL IS IN THE DETAILS

Have you ever drunk something in a rush and had it go down the "wrong tube/pipe"? In that pivotal moment, time seems to slow down. Nothing seems important but trying to catch your next breath. At that very moment, nothing seems to be of priority or consequence aside from your breathing. Then, as quickly as you are able to get your breath back, you are back to worrying about your endless "to-do" lists and beating yourself up about some mistake you made in the near or distant past.

Yet, that very moment teaches us something vital: being present and laser-focused. The air in our lungs we took for granted was now pushed to the present, and all other concerns were flushed out of our minds immediately. So it is with mindfulness; we are teaching our students to return to the most constant and simplistic means of their existence, which is that of their breathing.

As an educator, with all of the academic requirements and stringent curriculum mandates, it can be hard to believe that something as simplistic as breathing can be so pivotal to students.

The activity of breathing an average of 20,000 times daily is a constant means of grounding us all in the present moment and has vital benefits within the classroom and beyond. Think of a student that has severe test anxiety: They breathe shallowly and fast and begin to have a panic attack, thus providing a feeling of impending that makes the production of work essentially impossible.[9] Studies indicate, in fact, that mindfulness breathing does show promising benefits in the aid of focus, anxiety, and fear of test-taking.[10] Additionally, it can boost mood, fatigue, and stress, which youth may not recognize as having an impact on their emotional regulation and ability to focus academically.[11]

TEACHING MINDFUL BREATHING TO OUR STUDENTS

With a discussion of the benefits of focused breathing on the emotional regulation and health of our students, the question becomes how do we apply this concept into the larger classroom setting? There are several means of mindful breathing techniques; keep in mind that many of these only take a few moments and can be applied when, and as many times, they are needed in a school day to get students to become refocused and disciplined to the focus of the current moment. The goal of each is to calm students by utilizing breathing as a means to stay present.

BREATHING TECHNIQUES FOR EARLY ELEMENTARY STUDENTS

Younger children tend to look at play and imagination as their workplace. Hence, they tend to be good at adapting their imagination to the world. Thus, utilizing breathing techniques that use such techniques are more easily used.

Dandelion Breathing

As children, many of us remember blowing on the dandelion flowers in which the cotton-like seeds would be taken by the wind and flown far away. This practice was usually accompanied by making a wish when blowing the seeds of the flower.

1. Have students take a deep breath.
2. Have students imagine blowing out the seeds of the dandelion.
3. Have them discuss the wishes that they would wish for in a morning SEL discussion.

Starfish Breathing

This breathing technique has an additional objective in that it also is tactile and helps the student to calm themselves down by grounding them to the situation at hand. Grounding refers in mindfulness practice to cues that help one stay within the present moment.[12] Have the student place their hand on a piece of paper and trace their fingers while taking a deep breath, inhaling through their nose as they trace up their finger, and exhaling through their mouth as they trace down each finger.

BREATHING TECHNIQUES ARE AS EASY AS 4-7-8

One of the simplest breathing techniques as educators we can utilize within a classroom setting is the 4-7-8 breathing technique. Students who are in a constant state of trauma are also, generally, in a constant state of "fight or flight." As we mentioned earlier, fight or flight takes the blood away from the brain, thus making it harder to concentrate or learn. The 4-7-8 technique activates the part of the nervous system that calms this reaction.[13] It has been found to have a host of benefits and has even been labeled as a "tranquilizer for the nervous system" by Dr. Andrew Weil, who is the creator of this form of breathing.[14]

Applying 4-7-8 Breathing

The technique of 4-7-8 breathing is relatively simple. That being noted, its application is no less useful.

- Have students place their tongues on the top of the roof of their mouths.
- Students will breathe in through their noses for the count of four.
- Have students hold their breath for a count of seven.
- Let the breath out completely for a count of eight.
- Continue this breathing pattern four times.
- The more students employ this method, the better it will work to decrease stressors.

MINDFULNESS IS ABOUT GRATITUDE

Our world has become flawed in terms of gratitude, and we are seeing the results in our classrooms as to what students expect, and we have fostered a society of entitlement. Whereas, in the past, parenting required the aspects of love, shelter, clothing, and food to be considered successful and complete, as parents, this is no longer the case. Now, the message somehow has been construed that students are also entitled to the latest clothing and technology as well.

The problem becomes that students solely seeking materialistic goals create more social discord and emotional unhappiness. For instance, if the student has received the latest smartphone, and believes they are the envy of all their peers, they will soon be knocked off their pedestal when their peer gets an even newer smartphone. Popularity, clothing, toys, and cars are all relative and leave students perpetually comparing themselves to their peers as a measure that they are successful and happy. In these cases, gratitude is pushed out of the way in support of what they have and others don't, or, alternatively, what they lack, and constant comparison with other peers is a recipe for self-esteem disaster.

GRATITUDE JOURNALING

Journaling has become a relatively abandoned practice that is going the way of cursive writing. Nevertheless, as an educator, we can integrate the concept of gratitude and mindfulness into our writing assignments. One only has to do it for 5 to 10 minutes daily, and it addresses SEL, mindfulness, and literary skills in a synergistic fashion. Having students jot down three to five things they are grateful for each day and, perhaps, having a discussion if they wish to share is all it takes.[15] Though this concept is simplistic, countless research has shown that students having awareness of gratitude decreases student anxiety and helps to foster stronger interpersonal relationships.[16]

MINDFULNESS AND WRITING SYNERGISTICALLY

One of the reasons why we are swayed away from conducting mindfulness and SEL lessons in the classroom is simply due to the fact that other more pressing academic issues put the idea of SEL/mindfulness on the back burner. Yet, if we can implement these concepts simultaneously, we can create a synergistic and positive impact in both domains. For instance, when we talk about mindfulness and gratitude, these are also perfect starts for writing prompts to use in a writing assignment. With the right prompt, we can do a great deal of mindfulness work and sharpen a student's writing skills.

The following are some useful writing prompts that garner the best of writing, mindfulness, and gratitude.[17]

- Who do you consider your best role model? Why?
- If you were president for a day, what would you do?
- If you could take an imaginary vacation anywhere, where would it be? What would it be like?
- Think about one person who cares about you. How do they show they care?
- What is the most important thing you learned in school this year?
- What are three things that make you proud of who you are?
- If you had a magic wand and could make three wishes, what would they be? Why?

DO A MINDFULNESS SCAVENGER HUNT

Mindfulness is primarily about being present in the moment. It is about not focusing on the past or the future. Unfortunately, many of our students are in the emotional purgatory of these two worlds, which leads to frustration, anxiety, or sadness about not being able to change the future or past. A primary means of addressing this is to be aware of the minor details of what is around you at the moment, such as the following:

- What are five things you see in the room that you did not notice before?
- What are four things you can feel in the room (i.e., hot, cold, breezy, calm, lightness, darkness)?
- What are three things you can smell in the room right now?
- What is something you may be able to taste now in your mouth?[18]

THE MAGIC WAND AND THE THREE WISHES

In chaotic households, often times the student's wishes, thoughts, or opinions are pushed away as parents just struggle to keep the family afloat. This technique, adopted from Brief Solution Focused Therapy, can help a student to develop gratitude skills and shine a light on other elements of the student's social and emotional state.[19] It simply asks a student, "If you had a magic wand and could have three wishes, what would they be?"

These wishes could be modified to three wishes for their home, school, friends, family, and so on. Also, the savvy student will wish for more wishes, which are restricted in this particular exercise. The answers will often help to determine desires for social interactions, family closeness, or what supports they feel are lacking for them socially or emotionally in school or at home.

IF YOU WERE PRINCIPAL FOR THE DAY

A similar activity to the preceding one is having students answer how they would change school if they were the principal for a day. Not only does this provide a barometer of school climate, but it also can provide valuable insight into how the student sees their place socially and emotionally within the larger school context. This also provides students a means of something they long for: the ability to be listened to and control.

Chapter 6

Conclusion

The purpose of school is not to help kids do well in school . . . the purpose of school is to help kids do well in life.

—Eliot Eisner

Social-emotional learning (SEL) is, without a doubt, one of the most important lessons we can teach our students in the educational realm. As educators, we must be careful not to be myopic and see only what daily academics bring. We often discuss the long-term goal of vision, which can be extremely difficult when we are drowning in the procedure of the day, which seems to grow exponentially every year. Statistics and data we are told guide many of these decisions, but what of SEL and the statistics in that domain?

It is found that those children who received an SEL curriculum in kindergarten had fewer emotional issues and less chance of substance abuse and promiscuous behaviors at age 25 versus those who did not.[1] These are not statistics that we can ignore in the larger scope of student success. Schools must look at standardized scores in conjunction with standards of mental health and societal successes.

We have seen the scourge of school shootings and other types of violence that occur ever more frequently and have no sign of ceasing. Further, bullying and cyberbullying now have stronger new laws, and yet they do not abate. Still, when the media provides a profile of the most violent students, we see some stark similarities. They tend to be males who report being bullied from an early age. These students are frequently withdrawn and exist on the fringes of school society, having few, if any, friendships.[2] Further, they feel that the imagined injustices that they have received have led to the violence that they deliver, and this vengeance is their only avenue.

Interviews with those who knew the student often specify that little was known about the student. Descriptors like "strange," "outcast," "different," "kept to himself," and "loner" are often associated with these students. Yet, these students often don't get the help they need because they don't overtly show signs of their troubled nature in a manner that would create significant behavioral issues or school infractions, until they do so in an extreme and violent manner.

SEL is certainly not the panacea to addressing what is a complex and difficult societal, psychological, and political issue. That being said, mental health and social-emotional health do go hand-in-hand. Students who feel less alone and who know how to handle their anger and frustration are overall healthier individuals that can contribute to society. Looking at mental health as a public health and public education issue prioritizes the need to help students as a whole versus those who show only aggressive tendencies, which may go a long way toward making society a more habitable and kinder place.

Throughout the nation, schools teaching SEL have increased the amount of funding that has been spent in this area by roughly 45% between the period of November 2019 and April 2021.[3] Further, most schools are spending upwards of $100 per student on curriculum specific to SEL, following federal funding from COVID-19.[4] These are promising developments; however, it is important that we recognize SEL has recently been lumped together with other, more controversial curriculum domains, such as critical race theory (CRT) and sexual education, thus becoming a source of controversy among certain segments of the public that are skeptical about public school teaching or anything related to social interactions.[5]

On the flip side, students that have in the recent past been socially isolated due to social distancing have had two years in which they have had lessened social interaction aptitude and skill. We know that students who are home for two months in the summer in third through fifth grade lose an average of 27% in math and 20% in reading aptitude.[6] What of students who have had two years of social distancing; what is the regression socially? Since we have never done this since perhaps the Spanish Influenza Outbreak of 1918, we simply do not have answers as to social and emotional consequences. Thus, we are in the midst of what is a grand experiment on how students handle social isolation for a significant period of time and transition back to public school and society.

We do have to be very careful of how we conduct SEL lessons in classrooms due to cultural differences. For instance, we say that no eye contact is evidence that one is not listening. Yet, in certain cultures, looking at your teacher directly in the eye is disrespectful. In some Eastern, Caribbean, and Asian cultures, eye contact is considered downright rude. In yet other cultures, it is sometimes recommended depending on circumstance, and in Western society, it is considered a necessity.[7] Therefore, we cannot say that one particular means of executing SEL or social-emotional interaction is appropriate or absolutely correct without also an understanding of the varying cultural norms.

What is crystal clear is that something must be done about social-emotional interactions. Students, as we mentioned earlier, have turned to social media and cybercommunication as their main forms of socializing. Friendship and socialization definitions have been radically altered in the last several years so that one can dismiss a so-called "friend" with the click of a button without any recognition of consequences. Students now have an ever-blurred line between in-person and internet relationships and don't understand the real consequences that each employs.

SEL in public schools is in its relative infancy since the term was coined in 1994 after professionals in bullying prevention, child development, emotional intelligence, and public health put their heads together to develop a means to enrich the child-based, whole-student approaches first established by John Dewey only a generation ago.[8] An organization to further bolster the advocacy in this cause was established that same year called CASEL (Collaborative for Academic, Social and Emotional Learning) to promote these important fundamental ideals.[9] In the last three decades, the constructs of SEL have continued to grow in acceptance and evolution. It is the hope that SEL will continue to grow alongside other school curricula as a necessary fundamental subject and develop better-rounded, emotionally healthy citizens that inherit the next century to come, with the creation of a kinder, emotionally smarter society.

WHERE DO WE GO WITH ALL OF THIS?

In schools and organizations, often, the discussion is of vision. Where is it that we want to go with all of our work 5, 10, or 15 years into the future? The hope is to develop students that have character and are emotionally mature. What does this look like?

1. **The ability to be resilient:** Students should grow to be able to have discipline and patience to reach the goals they need in life.
2. **Ability to take responsibility:** Students should be able to take the same degree of responsibility for the negatives and positives within their lives.
3. **Not needing to be the center of attention:** The recognition that they are not the only person in society and that they are a contributing member versus the only one.
4. **Humor:** Not taking themselves, or life, so cynically that they cannot survive without laughter.

5. **Self-esteem:** Believing in themselves without having an ego that overshadows empathy for others.
6. **Ability to forgive:** The notion that forgiving oneself and others is the key to relationships and mental health.
7. **Gratitude:** Students are happy with what they have versus perpetually wanting more.
8. **Ability to be your own best friend:** Instead of a constant need to be filled with the company of others, students should genuinely like themselves and be able to forge out on one's own.
9. **Handling anger appropriately:** The ability to state anger in a manner that is productive and is not destructive to self or others.
10. **Ability to empathize:** The ability to understand how others feel and take perspective from a view outside their own.

Notes

INTRODUCTION

1. Aggressive driving and road rage. (n.d.). SafeMotorist.com. Retrieved December 12, 2022, from https://www.safemotorist.com/Articles/road-rage/.

2. Spence, J. (2021, March 5). Nonverbal communication: How body language & nonverbal cues are key. *Lifesize*. Retrieved December 12, 2022, from https://www.lifesize.com/blog/speaking-without-words/.

3. Steinmetz, K. (2018, September 10). Teens are over face-to-face communication, study says. *Time*. Retrieved December 12, 2022, from https://time.com/5390435/teen-social-media-usage/.

4. What is social-emotional learning? (n.d.). Committee for Children. Retrieved December 12, 2022, from https://www.cfchildren.org/what-is-social-emotional-learning/.

5. Columbia University's Mailman School of Public Health. (2022, September 19). Nearly one in 10 in the US reports having depression: Prevalence is particularly high among adolescents and young adults. *ScienceDaily*. Retrieved December 12, 2022, from www.sciencedaily.com/releases/2022/09/220919122248.htm.

6. U.S. Department of Health and Human Services. (n.d.). Any anxiety disorder. National Institute of Mental Health. Retrieved December 12, 2022, from https://www.nimh.nih.gov/health/statistics/any-anxiety-disorder.

7. Twenge, J. M., & Campbell, W. K. (2001). Age and birth cohort differences in self-esteem: A cross-temporal meta-analysis. *Personality and Social Psychology Review*, 5(4), 321–44. https://doi.org/10.1207/S15327957PSPR0504_3.

8. Allison. (2014, February 27). The global economic cost of violence containment. The Peace Alliance. Retrieved December 12, 2022, from https://peacealliance.org/the-global-economic-cost-of-violence-containment/.

9. American Psychological Association. (n.d.). APA reaffirms position on violent video games and violent behavior. American Psychological Association. Retrieved December 12, 2022, from https://www.apa.org/news/press/releases/2020/03/violent-video-games-behavior.

10. Cyberbullying statistics and facts for 2022. (2022, December 12). Comparitech. Retrieved December 12, 2022, from https://www.comparitech.com/internet-providers/cyberbullying-statistics/.

CHAPTER 1

1. hollowc2. (2022, December 9). What happens during fight or flight response. Cleveland Clinic. Retrieved December 12, 2022, from https://health.clevelandclinic.org/what-happens-to-your-body-during-the-fight-or-flight-response/.

2. Sussex Publishers. (n.d.). Parenting frustration in children: Aarrgghh! *Psychology Today.* Retrieved December 12, 2022, from https://www.psychologytoday.com/us/blog/the-power-prime/201009/parenting-frustration-in-children-aarrgghh.

3. Conrad, R. (2019). *Culture Hacks: Deciphering Differences in American, Chinese, and Japanese Thinking.* Austin, TX: Lioncrest Publishing.

4. Ibid.

5. Miller, Chris. (2021, September 22). The meaning of hand gestures around the World: English live blog. EF English Live. Retrieved December 6, 2022, from https://englishlive.ef.com/blog/english-in-the-real-world/hand-gestures/.

6. Kids offered coping skills at North Vegas School "Zen Den." (n.d.). US News. Retrieved December 12, 2022, from https://www.usnews.com/news/best-states/nevada/articles/2022-04-24/kids-offered-coping-skills-at-north-vegas-school-zen-den.

7. Henkel, V., Bussfeld, P., Möller, H. J., et al. (2002). Cognitive-behavioural theories of helplessness/hopelessness: Valid models of depression? *European Archives of Psychiatry and Clinical Neurosciences,* 252, 240–249. https://doi.org/10.1007/s00406-002-0389-y.

8. Darlene Lancer, J. D. (2018, June 30). Reality isn't always what you think! How cognitive distortions harm us. *Psych Central.* Retrieved December 16, 2022, from https://psychcentral.com/lib/reality-isnt-always-what-you-think-how-cognitive-distortions-harm-us#1.

9. Children and egocentrism—education gateshead. (n.d.). Retrieved December 13, 2022, from https://educationgateshead.org/wp-content/uploads/2021/09/3535b-JH-Children-And-Egocentrism.pdf.

10. Sussex Publishers. (n.d.). Frustration tolerance and its role in anger arousal. *Psychology Today.* Retrieved December 13, 2022, from https://www.psychologytoday.com/us/blog/overcoming-destructive-anger/202005/frustration-tolerance-and-its-role-in-anger-arousal.

11. Rath, T. (2017). *Strengthsfinder 2.0.* New York: Gallup Press.

12. Doukas, Thomas. (n.d.). Egocentrism beyond childhood—the Three Mountains. Retrieved December 15, 2022, from https://thomasdoukas.com/?p=21702.

13. *The Big Bang Theory: The Complete First Season.* (n.d.).

14. Sussex Publishers. (n.d.). Maslow's Hammer. *Psychology Today.* Retrieved December 16, 2022, from https://www.psychologytoday.com/us/blog/you-are-not-so-smart/201203/maslows-hammer.

15. Engelmann, J. M. & Tomasello, M. (2019). Children's sense of fairness as equal respect. *Trends in Cognitive Sciences*, 23, 454–463. https://doi.org/10.1016/j.tics.2019.03.001.

16. Supporting kids during a divorce. (2022, April 28). Child Mind Institute. Retrieved December 15, 2022, from https://childmind.org/article/supporting-kids-during-a-divorce/.

17. Steinbeis, N., Bernhardt, B. C., & Singer, T. (2012, March 8). Impulse control and underlying functions of the left DLPFC mediate age-related and age-independent individual differences in strategic social behavior. *Neuron*, 73(5), 1040–1051. doi:10.1016/j.neuron.2011.12.027. PMID: 22405212.

18. Bozzola, E., Spina, G., Agostiniani, R., Barni, S., Russo, R., Scarpato, E., Di Mauro, A., et al. (2022). The use of social media in children and adolescents: Scoping review on the potential risks. *International Journal of Environmental Research and Public Health*, 19(16), 9960. https://doi.org/10.3390/ijerph19169960.

19. Is nonverbal communication a numbers game? *Psychology Today*. Sussex Publishers. www.psychologytoday.com/us/blog/beyond-words/201109/is-nonverbal-communication-numbers-game.

20. Wolpert, S. (2018, March 12). In our Digital World, are young people losing the ability to read emotions? UCLA. Retrieved December 15, 2022, from https://newsroom.ucla.edu/releases/in-our-digital-world-are-young-people-losing-the-ability-to-read-emotions.

21. Mast, M. S., & Ickes, W. (2007). Empathic accuracy: Measurement and potential clinical applications. In T. Farrow & P. Woodruff (eds.), *Empathy in Mental Illness* (pp. 408–427). Cambridge: Cambridge University Press. doi:10.1017/cbo9780511543753.023.

22. Amabile, T., & Kramer, S. (2015). Inner work life: Understanding the subtext of business performance. *IEEE Engineering Management Review*, 43 (1), 43–51, doi:10.1109/emr.2015.7059374.

CHAPTER 2

1. Israelashvili, J., Sauter, D., & Fischer, A. (2019, October 21). How well can we assess our ability to understand others' feelings? beliefs about taking others' perspectives and actual understanding of others' emotions. Frontiers. Retrieved December 15, 2022, from https://www.frontiersin.org/articles/10.3389/fpsyg.2019.02475/full.

2. Bayless, K. (2022, October 12). What is helicopter parenting? Parents. Retrieved December 15, 2022, from https://www.parents.com/parenting/better-parenting/what-is-helicopter-parenting/.

3. Mischel, W., Zeiss, R., & Zeiss, A. (1974). Stanford preschool internal-external scale. PsycTESTS Dataset: n.p. Retrieved August 18, 2023, from https://pubmed.ncbi.nlm.nih.gov/957091/.

4. Ibid.

5. Duckworth, A. L., Peterson, C., Matthews, M. D., & Kelly, D. R. (2007). Grit: Perseverance and passion for long-term goals. *Journal of Personality and Social Psychology*, 92, 1087–1101.

6. Nicola. (2020, December 7). 12 steps to teaching your child perseverance. Minds of Wonder. Retrieved December 8, 2022, from https://mindsofwonder.com/2020/06/01/12-steps-to-teaching-your-child-perseverance/.

CHAPTER 3

1. How to answer "how are you?" around the world. Tandem. (n.d.). Retrieved December 19, 2022, from https://www.tandem.net/blog/how-are-you-around-the-world.

2. Social/emotional interventions: Teaching by rote or teaching by context? (2019, January 22). Inclusive Education Planning. Retrieved December 16, 2022, from https://inclusiveeducationplanning.com.au/uncategorized/social-emotional-interventions-teaching-by-rote-or-teaching-by-context/.

3. Jiménez, E. del, Alarcón, R., & de Vicente-Yague, M.-I. (2019). Reading intervention: Correlation between emotional intelligence and reading competence in high school students. *Revista De Psicodidáctica (English Ed.)*, 24(1), 24–30. https://doi.org/10.1016/j.psicoe.2018.10.001.

4. Kurt, D. S. (2021, January 30). Maslow's hierarchy of needs in Education. Education Library. Retrieved December 16, 2022, from https://educationlibrary.org/maslows-hierarchy-of-needs-in-education/.

5. Cai, X., Fan, Q., & Yuan, C. (2021, September 21). The impact of only child peers on the classroom environment and students' cognitive and non-cognitive outcomes. Available at https://ssrn.com/abstract=3927536 or http://dx.doi.org/10.2139/ssrn.3927536.

6. Swallow, D. (2014, April 28). Building social skills through play dates. North Shore Pediatric Therapy. Retrieved December 13, 2022, from https://www.nspt4kids.com/parenting/building-social-skills-through-play-dates/.

7. IAC Publishing. (n.d.). What is the origin of the phrase "it takes a village to raise a child"? Reference. Retrieved December 13, 2022, from https://www.reference.com/world-view/origin-phrase-takes-village-raise-child-3e375ce098113bb4.

8. Maslow, A. (n.d.). If you only have a hammer, you tend to . . . brainyquote. https://www.brainyquote.com/quotes/abraham_maslow_126079

9. Barron, C. (2015, May 18). How technical devices influence children's brains. *Psychology Today*. Sussex Publishers. Retrieved August 18, 2023, from https://www.psychologytoday.com/us/blog/the-creativity-cure/201505/how-technical-devices-influence-childrens-brains. 09 May 2017.

10. Jess, S. (2020, December 5). 5 introverted countries and cultures that value introversion. Introverted Growth. Retrieved December 13, 2022, from https://introvertedgrowth.com/5-introverted-countries-and-cultures-that-value-introversion/.

11. U.S. Department of Health and Human Services. (n.d.). Social anxiety disorder. National Institute of Mental Health. Retrieved December 21, 2022, from https://www.nimh.nih.gov/health/statistics/social-anxiety-disorder.

CHAPTER 4

1. Your child is likely to use trial and error methods now. (n.d.). Pregnancy Delivery Packages. Retrieved December 16, 2022, from https://www.parentlane.com/child/child-development/your-child-is-likely-to-use-trial-and-error-methods-now.

2. When (and why) kids are so brutally honest. (2022, April 5). Toddler Purgatory. Retrieved December 16, 2022, from https://www.toddlerpurgatory.com/when-and-why-kids-are-so-brutally-honest/.

3. Parenting, W. E. (2021, December 19). 3 ways to teach kids to be honest without being hurtful—wikihow mom. Retrieved December 16, 2022, from https://www.wikihow.mom/Teach-Kids-to-Be-Honest-Without-Being-Hurtful.

4. Mcleod, S. (n.d.). The preoperational stage of cognitive development. Piaget's Preoperational Stage (Ages 2–7): Definition, & Examples. Simply Psychology. Retrieved December 16, 2022, from https://www.simplypsychology.org/preoperational.html.

5. Krebs, D. (1975). Empathy and altruism. *Journal of Personality and Social Psychology*, 32 (6), 1134–1146, doi:10.1037/0022-3514.32.6.1134.

6. Konrath, S. H., et al. (May 2010). Changes in Dispositional Empathy in American College Students over Time: A Meta-Analysis. *Personality and Social Psychology Review*, 15 (2), 180–198, doi:10.1177/1088868310377395.

7. Brower, T. (2022, October 12). Think empathy is a soft skill? Think again. Why you need empathy for success. *Forbes*. Retrieved December 16, 2022, from https://www.forbes.com/sites/tracybrower/2019/06/16/think-empathy-is-a-soft-skill-think-again-why-you-need-empathy-for-success/?sh=7454a4ec76d6.

8. Boursier, V., Gioia, F., & Griffiths, M. D. (2020). Selfie-engagement on social media: Pathological narcissism, positive expectation, and body objectification—which is more influential? *Addictive behaviors reports*, 11, 100263. https://doi.org/10.1016/j.abrep.2020.100263.

9. Anderson, J. (2019, January 3). *The much-hated "helicopter parenting" style has surprisingly broad appeal*. Quartz. Retrieved December 16, 2022, from https://qz.com/1514079/much-hated-helicopter-parenting-style-is-surprisingly-popular.

10. Salovey and Mayer's emotional intelligence theory. (2020, July 14). Exploring your mind. Retrieved December 16, 2022, from https://exploringyourmind.com/salovey-mayers-emotional-intelligence-theory/.

11. Jensen, K. (2012, November 13). *Intelligence is overrated: What you really need to succeed*. Forbes. Retrieved December 16, 2022, from https://www.forbes.com/sites/keldjensen/2012/04/12/intelligence-is-overrated-what-you-really-need-to-succeed/?sh=7d321c8bb6d2

12. Salovey, P., et al. (2004).. *Emotional Intelligence: Key Readings on the Mayer and Salovey Model.* Port Chester, NY: National Professional Resources Inc./Dude Publishing.

CHAPTER 5

1. Alleyne, R. (2011, February 11). Welcome to the information age—174 newspapers a day. *The Telegraph.* Retrieved October 31, 2022, from https://www.telegraph.co.uk/news/science/science-news/8316534/Welcome-to-the-information-age-174-newspapers-a-day.html; Why it's so hard to pay attention, explained by science-fast company. (n.d.). Fast Company. Retrieved October 31, 2022, from https://www.fastcompany.com/3051417/why-its-so-hard-to-pay-attention-explained-by-science.

2. Lyness, D. A. (ed.). (2017, November). Mindfulness (for kids)—nemours kidshealth. KidsHealth. Retrieved October 31, 2022, from https://kidshealth.org/en/kids/mindfulness.html.

3. ADDitude Editors. (2022, July 13). ADHD statistics: New add facts and research. ADDitude. Retrieved October 31, 2022, from https://www.additudemag.com/statistics-of-adhd/.

4. Goleman, D. (2018, March 9). Want kids to succeed? teach them focus. LinkedIn. Retrieved November 1, 2022, from https://www.linkedin.com/pulse/want-kids-succeed-teach-them-focus-daniel-goleman/.

5. ScienceDaily editors. (2013, September 5). Mindfulness training improves attention in children. ScienceDaily. Retrieved November 1, 2022, from https://www.sciencedaily.com/releases/2013/09/130905202847.htm.

6. Kapalka, G. (2010). *Counseling Boys and Men with ADHD.* New York: Routledge.

7. Mindfulness and SEL: What's the difference? (2021, August 20). Edulastic Blog. Retrieved December 6, 2022, from https://edulastic.com/blog/mindfulness-and-sel/.

8. Lee, A. (2019, July 16). Powerful synergy: SEL and mindfulness working together. Mindful Schools. Retrieved December 6, 2022, from https://www.mindfulschools.org/research-and-neuroscience/powerful-synergy-sel-and-mindfulness-working-together/.

9. Philippot, P., Chapelle, G., & Blairy, S. (2002). Respiratory feedback in the generation of emotion. *Cognition and Emotion,* 16(5), 605–627, https://doi.org/10.1080/02699930143000392.

10. Cho, H., Ryu, S., Noh, J., & Lee, J. (2016). The effectiveness of daily mindful breathing practices on test anxiety of students. *PLOS ONE,* 11(10), e0164822. https://doi.org/10.1371/journal.pone.0164822.

11. *Breathing Exercises to Reduce Stress.* (n.d.). Healthy Place. Retrieved November 17, 2022, from https://www.healthyplace.com/alternative-mental-health/treatments/breathing-exercises-to-reduce-stress.

12. Nortje, A. (2022, December 8). 10+ mindful grounding techniques (incl. group exercise). PositivePsychology.com. Retrieved December 8, 2022, from https://positivepsychology.com/grounding-techniques/#grounding.

13. 4-7-8 breathing method for sleep and relaxation. (n.d.). Cleveland Clinic. Retrieved November 17, 2022, from https://health.clevelandclinic.org/4-7-8-breathing

14. Bulzoni, S. (2022, February 22). Breathing exercises: Three to try: 4-7-8 breath: Andrew Weil, M.D. DrWeil.com. Retrieved November 17, 2022, from https://www.drweil.com/health-wellness/body-mind-spirit/stress-anxiety/breathing-three-exercises/.

15. Gratitude journal for students. (n.d.). Greater Good in Action. Retrieved December 8, 2022, from https://ggia.berkeley.edu/practice/gratitude_journal_for_students.

16. Wood, A. M., et al. (2010, November). Gratitude and well-being: A review and theoretical integration. *Clinical Psychology Review*, 30 (7), 890–905, doi:10.1016/j.cpr.2010.03.005.

17. Bailey, K. (2018, July 5). 5 powerful health benefits of journaling. Intermountain Healthcare. https://intermountainhealthcare.org/blogs/topics/live-well/2018/07/5-powerful-health-benefits-of-journaling/.

18. Five senses worksheets PDF—free activities. (2022, April 25). Worksheets PDF. Retrieved December 16, 2022, from https://worksheetspdf.com/five-senses.

19. The "Magic wand" question. (2022, January 5). SOVA. Retrieved December 21, 2022, from https://sova.pitt.edu/the-magic-wand-question.

CHAPTER 6

1. Long-term benefits of social-emotional learning for at-risk students. (2019, June 3). ResilientEducator.com. Retrieved December 19, 2022, from https://resilienteducator.com/classroom-resources/sel-at-risk-students/.

2. Borba, M. (2009). *The Big Book of Parenting Solutions: 101 Answers to Your Everyday Challenges and Wildest Worries* (1st ed.). New York: Jossey-Bass.

3. Finding your place 2021. (n.d.). Retrieved December 19, 2022, from https://d1hzkn4d3dn6lg.cloudfront.net/production/uploads/2021/10/Tyton-Partners_Finding-Your-Place-2021_SEL-Takes-Center-Stage-in-K12.pdf.

4. National, regional trends in educators' covid-relief spending. (n.d.). FutureEd—A New Voice for American Education. Retrieved December 19, 2022, from https://www.future-ed.org/national-reading-trends-covid-relief-spending/.

5. Field, K. (2022, March 11). Social and emotional learning is the latest flashpoint in the education wars. The Hechinger Report. Retrieved December 20, 2022, from https://hechingerreport.org/social-and-emotional-learning-is-the-latest-flashpoint-in-the-education-wars/.

6. Map growth. NWEA. (2022, December 5). Retrieved December 19, 2022, from https://www.nwea.org/map-growth/.

7. Jordan, P. W., & DiMarco, B. (2022, March 1). National, regional trends in educators' covid-relief spending. FutureEd. Retrieved August 18, 2023, from https://www.future-ed.org/national-reading-trends-covid-relief-spending/.

8. George Lucas Educational Foundation. (2011, October 7). Social and Emotional Learning: A short history. Edutopia. Retrieved December 21, 2022, from https://www.edutopia.org/social-emotional-learning-history.

9. Advancing social and emotional learning. (2022, October 14). CASEL. Retrieved December 21, 2022, from https://casel.org/#:~:text=Collaborative%20for%20Academic%2C%20Social%2C%20and%20Emotional%20Learning%20(CASEL),Systemic%20Implementation.

About the Author

Dr. Brett Novick holds a bachelor's degree in psychology from LaSalle University in Philadelphia, Pennsylvania, and a master's degree in family therapy from Friends University in Wichita, Kansas, as well as post-degree work and certification in school social work from Monmouth University in West Long Branch, New Jersey, and a doctorate in educational leadership from American College of Education in Indianapolis, Indiana. Dr. Novick is licensed as a marriage and family therapist and state-certified as a school social worker, supervisor, principal, and educational administrator.

He has worked as a school social worker/counselor for the last 22 years and is an adjunct instructor at Rutgers University in New Brunswick, New Jersey. Additionally, he has been a licensed marriage and family therapist in private practice, community mental health, and substance abuse settings over the last 20 years. Additionally, he has supervised family counseling, school counseling, and centers for abused and neglected children as well as adults and children with developmental disabilities.

He has authored national and international articles in the *American Association of Marriage and Family Therapy*, *Autism Parenting*, *National Education Digest*, *NJEA Review*, *National Association of Special Education Teachers*, *NASSP Principal Leadership*, *Better Mental Health*, and *ASCD Educational Leadership* magazines. He has authored four additional books: *Parents and Teachers Working Together* (2016) and *The Likable, Effective, and Productive Educator* (2017), both published by Rowman & Littlefield; *Don't Marry a Lemon* (2017); and *Brain Bullies: Standing Up to Anxiety and Worry* (2017). Additionally, he is the creator of three therapeutic children's games.

He has been humbled with numerous awards for his work in education, inclusive education, counseling, character education, and human rights. These include the NJEA Martin Luther King Jr. Human and Civil Rights Award, the NJSCA Ocean County School Counselor of the Year Award, the Ocean County Mental Health Advocate Award, the NJ Council on Developmental

Disabilities Community Award, the NJ DOE Holocaust Educator Hela Young Award, the NJ DOE Inclusive Educator of the Year and Exemplary Educator Awards, NJSCA Human Rights Advocate Award, ETS/Kids Bridge Character Educator of the Year Award, and the US Congressional Recognition for Community Service.

www.ingramcontent.com/pod-product-compliance
Lightning Source LLC
Chambersburg PA
CBHW030241170426
43202CB00007B/83